DUSTY

DUSTY

"Scissors and Paste"

A Collage Biography

A personal appreciation
of the life and career of
Dusty Springfield.

BRITANNIA PRESS PUBLISHING

Copyright © Evans. 1995

First published in Great Britain by Britannia Press Publishing, 1995.
This edition published in 1995 by Britannia Press Publishing.

British Library Cataloguing in Publication Data. A catalogue record for this
book is available from the British Library.

    Evans
    Scissors and Paste - A Collage Biography
    A Personnal Appreciation of the Life and Career
    of Dusty Springfield

    ISBN 0-9519937-7-1

Printed and bound in Great Britain by WBC, Bridgend
Cover photograph: Rex Features

Britannia Press Publishing, 72 Chalk Farm Road, London NW1 8AN.
Mail Orders, PO Box 3496, London NW1 SD0.

This book is dedicated to the memory of
CHERRY BROWN
who died in 1993
She was the same age as Dusty

And to Joe Fanelli, Peter Allen, Edward Duke,
Douglas Goodall, James Monks and Dennis Lemon.
My thanks too to Mike Gill and David Minns.

Acknowledgements

I could not have written this book without having access to Dusty's quoted words. Instead of annotating each quote separately which interrupted the text, I prefer to acknowledge en bloc the journalists and organs of the media who are the sources of the quotations:

Lucy O'Brien and her biographical work DUSTY, Chris Heath and GIRL ABOUT TOWN, Mike Nicholls and HELLO! Magazine, John Selby, Chrissie Iley, Laura Lee Davies, INITIAL FILMS, BBC RADIO 2, Keith Howes and GAY NEWS, NEW MUSICAL EXPRESS, "Q" Magazine, Pete Goodman, Don Short, RECORD MIRROR, Marcelle Bernstein and THE OBSERVER, Sharon Davis, Adam Sweeting and THE GUARDIAN, Marcus Greil and ROLLING STONE, Penny Valentine and DISC, Chris White and MUSIC WEEK, Peter Evans, Ray Coleman, Dave Gelly, Graham Lock, The REPUTATION Video, CASHBOX and THE DAILY MAIL.

To the persons mentioned above I am indebted for eliciting Dusty's words. To the organs mentioned we are indebted for making these words known.

Final thanks to Pat Rhodes. What a friend!

INTRODUCTION

Dusty Springfield's has turned out to be the voice of a generation. The sound of it lends identity to some very special wonder years. Dusty's is a voice which is inimitable. Inimitable means that it defies imitation. Over the thirty years of Dusty's solo career, the voice and its owner may have been parodied, lampooned and impersonated but I have never heard any convincing imitation of Dusty's voice.

In 1963, the year that President Kennedy was assassinated and the cynics finally took over the world, Dusty Springfield was one of several contenders. She shared the wings with three significant peers, Lulu, Cilla Black and Sandie Shaw.

Lulu had bounce and zing and was vaultingly ambitious. She sang very loudly and, like Israel's trumpets at Jericho, breached the walls of the entertainment establishment who embraced her effervescent wholesomeness with open arms. She married politically, if not eternally. She had strong and continuous management in the person of Marion Massey - Lulu was always to be found and you always got an answer back. However, the voice itself was not unique. People do it very convincingly on STARS IN THEIR EYES on Saturday nights.

Cilla was a very nice girl. Everybody said so at the time and it is patently a home truth. Homely was and is Cilla's byword. Beneath its comfortable umbrella, she presented no threat as 'our Cilla' patiently waited to inherit the Britannic mantle divested by Gracie Fields when 'our Gracie' settled on Capri. Cilla sang with a deceptive emotion and a gargling vibrato for the sound of the songs was just that, sound. There was little substance. I never felt that Cilla was hurting. She was elegant and modish and stood still rather effectively but the qualities that will eventually enable her to become the Queen Mum of

The Biz were the ones that secured the audience when she and her post-Epstein show-business associates began to market her personality. As well as having Brian Epstein as her manager, she also had Bobby Willis and when Brian left her and us, she still had Bobby. And she still has Bobby. Like Lulu, Cilla's career has enjoyed a continuously stable infrastructure. The voice still exists as witnessed by her recent duet on HEART AND SOUL with Dusty as well as her own thirtieth anniversary celebrations on television. But when you close your eyes, you now see rather than hear Cilla.

Sandie Shaw had style and sophistication and sang Chris Andrews' bubble-gum material with contemporary elegance. The voice was hard but flexible enough to run the register but somehow the sound of it ultimately grated as it reached its sell-by date. Sandie too married, badly and sadly as it turned out. She didn't manage to become a negotiable personality like Lulu or Cilla and, according to her autobiography, still bears the scars of the battle she did with her regrets and disappointments. In her own book, she writes about her management in not the most trusting of terms and her voice, ultimately, was not what it seemed. It seemed that a girl had been taken out of Dagenham but never was the Dagenham to be taken out of the woman the girl turned into and who could never go back.

Dusty wasn't alone in those distant nineteen sixty some-things - Susan Maughan, Twinkle of whom much more should be written and will be in later work, Helen Shapiro who had her day, Kathy Kirby, Julie Rogers, Shirley Bassey who was socking it to a different audience and had been for a decade, Petula Clark who was sensibly to emigrate, Marianne Faithful who was to have a well-deserved renaissance, Joan Baez, Brenda Lee even, Lesley Gore who went on to write ... These careers are undeniable but the voices are as indistinguishable nowadays - should any of them ever sing anything new - as are the voices of so many discocratic women who seem to emerge to rapturous acclaim for a brief spurt of incandescent celebrity and then recede into an invisible retro-life of sampled limbo.

Only a mad person would sample a Dusty Springfield vocal. You'd know who was singing in an instant and the samplers would get the shit sued out of them.

Since first hearing those searing Dusty ballads in the halcyon long ago, those of us who have been spared have all aged, we have all withered and the intervening thirty odd years have condemned all our fancied colouring books, willy-nilly, to sporting tones of browns and taupes and beiges and lovat. However, there are, stubbornly, a few patches of green still to be found on the wintry palettes of our dis- or con-tent and one of those green things for me is the voice of Dusty Springfield. Forever green.

So what is this thing about Dusty, which not only still intrigues us but also must intrigue her? Contrary to our expectations and her pronouncements, it seems she is set, as I write, to record once again. Sony, the record company, is still prepared to invest millions to own the voice in the sincere belief, obviously, that there are sufficient punters out there who will want to buy the voice and furnish Sony the profit on their millions. The record industry is canny like that. It seems to have employed far more and better accountants lately than it has done artists. Perhaps things are on the up? Unlike ourselves and unlike the artists who sing for us, it seems the record industry can't afford to make mistakes.

So, what is this thing about Dusty?

DUSTY

"I think I'm going back ..."

In her autobiography, THE LONELY LIFE, the film actress Bette Davis claimed that she acted better if she was in love. Since she frequently was, perhaps she did.

Love is a commodity we all need and yet, illogically, we can't buy. It seems a strange commodity on which to found a civilisation for it is, after all, the mutual love between a man and a woman which is supposed to be the fundament of marriage and it is beneath the marriage umbrella that most of us saw our first light of day.

Not only can we not buy love, but, to add insult to injury, we cannot rely on it when it comes our way. Though we are brought up to be dependent on it, it seems that it is its very absence which has the more powerful influence on our infant, childhood, teenage and adult lives. And, just to complicate matters, love comes in so many forms, so many guises and each one is equally important but has to synchromesh smoothly and effortlessly with all the others in order to be at all functional. Love turns us all to addicts. We're each of us dependants and there's no chemical substitute.

Perhaps if we were taught both by example and lesson from the first moments of our lives to do without love, we would be better empowered to more healthily control and direct those lives out in the big, bad, real world. Might we then be pleasantly

1

- even ecstatically - surprised and pleased when love comes along but yet not quite so devastated when it ups and leaves us?

However, it seems that we're stuck with the dependency thing for the foreseeable future and thus we have to deal with it if we are going to be unable to understand both our own lives and the life and career of Dusty Springfield. Without love and without being without love, Dusty Springfield would never have existed at thirteen, twenty three, fifty three or, god willing, eighty three.

It seems superfluous to chronicle the facts of Dusty's childhood once again and yet it is niggardly not to do so for the edification of those who may be coming newly recruited to the ranks.

Dusty was born the second and youngest child of Kay and Gerard O'Brien. Dusty has recently claimed her birthplace was Somata Road. In Lucy O'Brien's (no relation) book DUSTY, the birthplace was at 87 Fordwych Road, West Hampstead in Northwest London. Both events, I hope, at least took place on the same day, the sixteenth of April 1939. Lauderdale Mansions in Maida Vale was another O'Brien residence, according to Dusty. Anyway, she started off as a London girl. What was to happen to her in life was mostly right on her doorstep or at least no further than a tube or bus ride away and without London, it hardly needs pointing out that Dusty Springfield would probably never have existed.

Kay and Gerard's eldest child, christened Dion, had been born four years previously when Kay was thirty five, four years after her marriage. Their newborn little girl was christened Mary Isobel Catherine Bernadette and baptised into the Roman Catholic Church.

If the first is love, the second most important necessity to adult human life would appear to be hindsight. Sadly, like love, hindsight is not a commodity you can buy four pennyworth of at the candy counter and that's a bugger because at the moment, I could do with a full pound bag. Probably Dusty too, for in all our lives we seem to need more of the stuff than even the air we breathe.

From what I can glean and from a lovely day spent with Pat Rhodes, Dusty's friend and helpmate for almost thirty five

2

years, it would appear that Mary's mother Kay, a first generation arrival from the Republic of Ireland, was somewhat volatile
whilst her father Gerard (known as OB - 'Obie'), who worked
a nine to five with companies' accounts, was more stable. That
he would have had to have been, both holding down his job and
getting up in the mornings would seem to bear ample witness.

Kay O'Brien was prone to staying up very late at night.
Being Irish, she was a lover of the crack'. She gave, by all
accounts, wonderful parties. She had or had had ambitions to be
an entertainer herself and was often involved in local amateur
dramatics. I would imagine the mother/daughter relationship
became one of the world's ready examples of wish fulfilment.
OB, had he had a choice, apparently had aspirations to be a
concert pianist. Coming to motherhood late and being the
character she reputedly was, one concludes that Dion and
Mary's mum didn't initially embrace the maternal role with
open arms. One of Mary's grandfathers was or had been an Irish
journalist, the parliamentary correspondent for the Irish Times.
Obviously a man of opinions, it would seem that Kay would
have been of similarly strong opinions herself. Dusty recently
made reference to other ancestors, her great-grandparents were
members of a travelling Gilbert and Sullivan company (an Irish
d'Oyly Carte or the British original?) Further Irish ancestry
comes over in Dusty's version as confused. But history for the
Irish plays an even greater part than the present. Bees somehow
seem to get more easily into Irish bonnets and find it harder to
escape. If Kay was explosive, Dusty remembers her father OB
as the opposite.

*"I was born in Hampstead and my father was a bit posh.
He went to a good school. He was born in India. The poor fellow
was shoved off to a public school in Derbyshire at the age of
seven. He'd go back to India for the holidays. The boat went so
slowly that he must have had time only for a plate of curry before
it was time to turn round and go back to school again. No
wonder he was so very shy and withdrawn all his life. In some
ways I take after him."*

OB had obviously seen something of the wider world and
been influenced by those voyages and sojourns in the cosmo-
politan foreign compounds of the fading British Empire. So,

given her later wanderlust, also stemming according to Dusty from a deeper historic family background in the Celtic mists as travelling tinkers, perhaps one part of Mary was inherently sourced from OB's spring of influence. The other part, the emotive side, seems definitely maternally inherited and as elastic and unpredictable as an elephant at the end of a bungee rope.

"My mother was given to slapping trifles very hard with a large spoon and saying, 'You're going to get it quicker this way'. In our house, things developed - out of an innocent slice of spam being lobbed across the room - into an absolute melee."

Sad to report but the O'Brien's marriage was not happy. I'm not surprised or amazed. Many of us have been born of marriages which weren't ideal but survived, struggling, because they fell short of being inimical. Dion and Mary were brought up in the nineteen forties and, what's more, Kay and OB were Catholic and you just didn't - in their case, couldn't - divorce. So, the children, like many children then and since, were heirs and party to some livid domestic rows and arguments. Very confusing for a child, unable to sleep, sitting at the top of the stairs in tearful, silent consternation listening to its parents screaming threats at each other's throats in a downstairs room. Despite the presence of a sibling, in Mary's case an elder brother, there is no communication cord in that compartment for the child to pull and so each child suffers the row as best as chance will have it and hopes the train will get to the next station as quickly as possible.

Child thinks: '*... Why is mummy screaming at daddy? Why does daddy call mummy such horrid names? Don't they love each other? Do they love me? ...*'

And what, indeed, of love itself as the concept clarifies in the child's developing mind? Something to be afraid of, perhaps? Something to be wary of, something not to be trusted after all?

Child thinks: '*... is it the same love I'm supposed to have for God and for Jesus? And if mummy doesn't love daddy, does Jesus really love me? ... Please make them stop.*'

What children learn or copy or inherit from their parents is obviously of huge importance to their development and future

4

ability to function. What they learn, copy and absorb from the influences of their extra-domestic environment is probably of greater importance. It is, however, the interaction of both spheres of influence which ultimately shapes us all.

For a child, the two spheres are usually home and school. If you are born with no arms, you are unlikely to be hit by your fellow schoolchildren and your armless talents will blossom elsewhere. But you will need and want to compensate to make your mark for the world will find other ways to be cruel to you. So, if you are born with an ability to sing, it is most likely you are going to be asked at some point sooner or later to do so in front of an audience. If you sing very well, it is likely you will be encouraged to concentrate on that talent either by proud parents or by enthusiastic teachers. Finally, Having thus made your compensating mark, you might not want to make any others, albeit to the detriment of the development of other qualities which are equally but perhaps not as urgently important to you. Every step we take is a sacrifice to the step we didn't take always regretting the steps we didn't take. What we have is in some cases less important than what we DON'T have because we spend more time wanting what we don't have rather than acknowledging and developing what we do.

"I liked history, geography, French and English. Struggled to GCE but I got a hate on about English because the book they gave me to read was Mansfield Park which I didn't like. I was too wrapped up in Budd Shulberg."

Dusty liked it, was probably good at it but 'got a hate on about English' because she didn't want what she had; she wanted more, what she didn't, yea couldn't, have. Interesting too that Dusty remembers reading an American book by an American author. Shulberg, whose chef d'oeuvre was WHAT MAKES SAMMY RUN, wrote extensively about Hollywood and its cine-infamous inhabitants and it would seem that the schoolgirl Mary frequently accompanied her mother Kay to the movies and that their favourite films were the Hollywood musicals of the early nineteen fifties. There were dozens of them. I name a lot of them merely to point out how influential this medium was ... Doris Day in CALAMITY JANE, Betty Hutton, Vera Ellen in THREE LITTLE WORDS and WHITE CHRISTMAS, Betty Grable in WARBASH AVENUE, Grace Kelly in THE COUNTRY GIRL and HIGH SOCIETY, Joan Blondell in THE BLUE VEIL, Marilyn Monroe in AS YOUNG AS YOU FEEL, GENTLEMEN PREFER BLONDES and HOW TO MARRY A MILLIONAIRE as well as THERE'S NO BUSINESS LIKE SHOW BUSINESS with Ethel Merman, Debbie Reynolds in SINGING IN THE RAIN, Lana Turner in THE MERRY WIDOW, Virginia Mayo in SHE'S WORKING HER WAY THROUGH COLLEGE, Catherine Grayson and Ann Miller in KISS ME KATE, Zsa Zsa Gabor in LILI and MOULIN ROUGE, Cyd Charisse in BAND WAGON, Judy Garland in A STAR IS BORN, Doris Day in LOVE ME OR LEAVE ME, Jean Simmons in GUYS AND DOLLS, Dolores Gray in KISMET, Shirley Jones in OKLAHOMA, Jane Powell, Debbie Reynolds and Ann Miller in HIT THE DECK ...

Mary was weaned on the best; her education was seminal and was Hollywood's apotheosis. Mary's stars in her teenage heaven were immutable, eternal, monolithic shibboleths, yet at the same time very, very real. Not only was life on the screen in Technicolour and spoken in ster-e-o-phonic sound, a lot of it was lived AND SUNG by huge, larger-than-life shimmering blondes. No wonder that in Mary's school, the black and white penguins couldn't manage to get Jane Austen to weather the technicolour competition and what a shame Mary's teacher had to stick to the curriculum.

Britain as a nation had been irrevocably Americanised by the arrival of the U.S. troops and air personnel during the second world war. No longer were Americans merely flickering images from 'over there' on our silver screens. They were real life flesh and blood men and women and they were 'over here' and, by god, weren't they attractive? They brought their bubble-gum and their nylons and their records and their dancing and their sex and a whole generation of women fell for them; many thousands even fell in love and when the time to came to leave, left with the conquering heroes.

And these American neo-gods were all and each so different; America was a rich nation not only in monetary terms but in the fabric of its hugely diverse culture, a sumptuous, vital, racial and ethnic tapestry bound not by traditional class frontiers but limited only by what an individual could achieve on their own. The American dream became the British hope in the dark days of rationing and deprivation following a bleak and cruel war which hadn't ended for the civilian population in 1945 at all but which dragged relentlessly on into the early fifties. Sacrifice was piled on sacrifice. America was what COULD have been. Britain became a nation of wannabees.

The British clutched at America and all things American. Unbeknownst to her, Mary O'Brien needed the vernacular and very twentieth century American Mr. Shulberg as her set text much more than she needed the socially refined nineteenth century good manners of a bygone and irrelevant English age.

But vernacular also means secular and Mary's teachers were unlikely collaborators. Mary's teachers had always been, and would always be, nuns.

By the time she was attending St. Anne's Convent School in Ealing, Mary had already attended St. Augustine's Roman Catholic Primary school and St. Bernard's Convent in High Wycombe, a town some thirty miles west of London to where Kay and OB had moved in 1949 when Mary was ten. Her whole secular education had been both underpinned and overshadowed by religion. I hate to be obvious but allowing children nowadays to watch video nasties is as nought compared to instilling tender ten year olds with vicious visions of eternal damnation, visions complete with the flames of everlasting torture. Seems odd that in order to focus the child's unformed perspective upon the face of god, it was deemed proper for that child's sensibilities to be instilled with threats of devils.

There are many wonderful books on growing up Catholic, notably Michael Carson's SUCKING SHERBERT LEMONS. Mr. Carson speaks eloquently of the pressures to which his teenage boy hero is subjected and similarly the young Mary O'Brien must have been subject to the same pressures to grow up to be a good and godly girl. And demure, and respectful and obedient and as free of sin and vice as humanly possible and, if sinful and prone to vice, (way to go, Satan!) then made to feel as guilty as all get out. The motto of St. Anne's, Ealing was GOODNESS IS EXCELLENCE. Being good in a Catholic context is just not on or there would be no room for sin and therefore no need for the religion and no point in being Catholic. Surely, St.

Anne's was rather a cruel motto? Significantly, the school no longer exists. Perhaps if its motto had been EXCELLENCE IS GOODNESS, it might still be there. I think Mary O'Brien and Dusty Springfield could have gone for that.

However, talking in 1970, Dusty was still mindful of her unpaid Catholic account:

"I still think that because I don't any longer (go to Mass), I'm going to hell ... But I don't want to go to hell because I haven't really done anything evil. I'm just lazy and self-indulgent."

Speaking years further on, Dusty seems to have come to terms with those early influences:

"It took me a while to forget all the stupidity connected with that set of morals. Okay, it works for some people and that's great. My mother, for instance, was a very good Catholic and it worked for her. But it doesn't work for people who constantly question it because there are no answers. And I can't accept that. I want answers. So I have my own form of faith now. It's just that it's not religious as such. Have you seen STAR WARS? Well, as in that film, I believe there's a force of some kind. And that works for me."

The age difference between Dion and Mary cannot have been that comforting initially and being the younger sibling to a high-achieving elder - and a brother to boot - obviously had an enormous effect. Mary found herself being emulative from an early age. I believe the comparative - and therefore the competitive streak - is still strong in Dusty and mainly responsible for her propensity to be overly self-critical.

"I wasn't very good at anything at school. I was at a convent school and the nuns were terribly strict and the standards terribly high. My brother passed fourteen subjects with honours. I left at fifteen, the first moment I could. I just wasn't that kind of bright. It was too much for me. I used to get very upset that I wasn't good enough. I was constantly comparing myself to him (Dion/Tom) and the feeling of inadequacy followed me through my life. Now I'm grateful to my brother because it was he who unwittingly started me off singing. I started because he started and I wanted to be better than him at something ... I was a very emotional teenager. I used to get terribly upset. I'm

still a very emotional person ... I felt I had to purge myself. I can see that confessing the truth is cleansing. But I used (at school) to make things up just to make sure that I WAS cleansed. That backfired on me terribly, they never let you forget it ..."

Dion's presence in her life was, however, more than just as an elder brother.

"I often wonder whether if Tom had wanted to be a vet, I would have wanted to be one too. But it was music. And he being four or five years older than me, I always wanted to play instruments as well as him and sing like him. I furiously tried to keep up with him."

There was criticism too which bombarded her childhood at school and, proportionately at home. Teenage seems to have bequeathed Dusty an excessive amount of self-doubt.

"I was always accused of being a very ungrateful child. 'It will show on your face one day, my child', my mum used to say. It was there in the scowl ..."

Over-criticised children tend to become self-critical children and grow up to be very aware; they can become very isolated, acting a lot on their own, apparently out of context, setting their own rules, making themselves less vulnerable to being judged by standards applicable to 'the majority'. Some could even be called devious, learning that to dissemble is often the most effective way of ducking out. I know.

By fifteen, Mary was obviously not going to be 'playing the game'. Being co-operative, because it was an expected virtue, was not on the menu.

"I function best, rather unfortunately, out of defiance," she admitted to Chris Heath in 1990.

She had been called Dusty for some time although by the end of her teenage, and even into the incarnation of THE SPRINGFIELDS, Mary O'Brien had not yet constructed Dusty Springfield as an alter ego or if she had done, Dusty had not yet made her entrance.

"I've had it (the name Dusty) since childhood. You see I was a bit of a tomboy and my friends thought that Dusty was an appropriate nickname for a girl who liked to play football in the streets with the boys ... No! I don't play anymore. I retired gracefully at fifteen!"

She was to leave school at the earliest possible moment when she was fifteen. Looking in the mirror on her last day at school, Mary's reflection was one with which she decided she could not and would not identify.

"... (there) was kind of a blob ... sort of overweight with national health glasses, played hockey ... but inside I was a seething mass of ambition, ready to claw my way to the top ... No, what was going on inside me was Twentieth Century Fox musicals. When no one was looking, I was leaping off desks doing Gene Kelly routines. I really wanted to be Cyd Charisse but I have very short legs. I knew something would happen to me, good or bad. I was not going to be a radiographer or a nurse."

The reflection in the mirror would have been slightly blurred as Mary was badly myopic. Whether she compensated for that aberrative image in her self-assessment is only my conjecture.

Her contemporaries at school claim they remember the teenage Mary proclaiming that she was indeed not going to become a radiographer or a nurse but that she was going to be a blues singer. Singing, other than with or without Dion at home, had already raised its head as a future avenue. At school, Mary sang in a three girl vocal group which was a little too raunchy in its musical proclivity for nunnish sensibilities. Their blues offering at a school concert was banned.

"I grew up listening to Ella Fitzgerald. I was singing Rogers and Hart songs when I was ten ..."

As well as classical music, OB was also a jazz fan and, listening, Dusty became familiar with the likes of Jelly Roll Morton.

"... I always used to say the same thing: 'I want to be a blues singer.' God knows what that meant ... I thought it would be appropriate. Besides that, I had a fierce crush on Peggy Lee's voice. That's who I wanted to be. I wanted to be Peggy Lee."

It seemed that singing presented itself as the only viable alternative to a fifteen year old school leaver in 1954-1955. In fact the young Mary would have been excluded from the secretarial or the nursing or the librarian options she maintains were alternatives because of her lack of qualification as much as her lack of motivation. If she had chosen not to go on to technical or secretarial college, shop work or unskilled factory work lay before her if she did not run with the singing. Nothing wrong with any of that work as is well-known but ... for Dusty?

"I get fits of being articulate followed by fits of being a complete and utter idiot. But I was encouraged to become a singer as neither of my parents were very routine people."

If singing had been a 'proper' job and had she been able to interview for a singing career the day she left school, her prospective employers would have auditioned an awkward girl who had not learned to make anything of her natural attributes. She had grown up uncertain and defensive. She was a girl whom some might have considered, wilful, even rude. She was a girl who burned on a very short fuse, a soul who acted more often emotionally rather than after due reflection and who had not even the adolescent temerity to allow what little experience she had accrued to compensate for impulse and temper.

Socially too, Mary was very sensitive for some reason. Later remarks illustrate her obvious dislike of social behaviour she considered pretentious or snobbish or patronising. She would probably have come across as worryingly unconfident and, occasionally, alarmingly prickly. The self-deprecation she has always displayed must have been more than evident then. This propensity was not merely ruthless self-criticism; it had already developed into obsessive self-put-down.

This miasma of character and psycho-baggage with which we emerge from the chrysalis of teenage and puberty is the same in quantity for all of us but in Mary O'Brien's case, its quality had borne a personality which had a swingeing fear of being overlooked, of being ordinary. Contradictorily, Mary needed to be noticed even though when she was, she often didn't want to be.

"It was a desire to get noticed. Which was strange because I was so shy. I mean, if I went to the pictures, I'd go in my school uniform. I didn't know how to dress up. I didn't know any different. It's a paradox, isn't it? It's almost as though I was schizophrenic."

Teenagers as a separate human sub-species, in 1954/55 were almost unidentifiable. It was very hard to be different or rebellious. Girls of sixteen mostly wore the same kind of clothes their mothers wore and mother and daughter shopping trips were quite normal. Saturday afternoons after work saw many a mother, daughter and even granny in the highstreet shops of the country towns.

Teenage life as such was confined. Mostly the pictures, occasionally church-based youth clubs, coffee bars if you lived in big cities and had avant garde parents, otherwise the street corners and clandestine dating whilst pretending to visit schoolfriends. But seeds of the schism between the generations had been sown. Rebellion was brewing, given face and voice by films like IT'S GREAT TO BE YOUNG with John Mills, Eleanor Summerfield and the ill-fated young actor Jeremy Spencer. Here was a whole school, admittedly pupilled by incredibly gifted orchestral musicians and singers, who stage strikes, sit-ins and mount passive resistance of all kinds in order to have their sacked music teacher re-instated. Being one of only a handful of British musicals, Mary and Kay must have seen it.

There was only one television channel, and only BBC radio's The Light Programme occasionally played music of teenage orientation which only very occasionally was specified as such. It was a world of theatre-based variety in the main, bland, music hall-derived 'family' entertainment performed on well-worn provincial theatrical circuits. Music as a separate arm of the entertainment industry had not yet developed. Hit popular music other than pappy ditties, warbled by Ann Shelton, came from Hollywood films.

I'm speaking generally. Particularly, it seemed that the O'Brien household was very, very different being musically rich, vibrant and varied. Obviously much influenced by things American, both Dion and Mary were not only conversant with but practising songs, rhythms and music from all over the world and knew something of the culture from which that music had sprung. Tom, so Dusty says, was passionate about Carmen Miranda and her backing band which in turn influenced her in her love of samba and all Brazilian, rhythm based music.

Of how much of the blues and gospel music and their traditions and history the O'Brien children were aware, I know not. It was definitely an awareness of both these musical caches which had already influenced Mary at an early age. She was fluent both in her understanding of the forms and her intentions to follow where this awareness led ... But did she know of the legendary gospeller Arizona Dranes who, blind, wandered from southern town to southern town almost with a begging bowl or the commercially more adept and sighted Robert Martin Singers from Chicago? Had she heard records by Ma Rainey and Bessie Smith? Had she indeed heard the contemporary work of Big Mama Thornton who sang Lieber and Stoller's HOUND DOG first in 1952? Did she know of Ruth Etting, Ethel Waters and Billie Holiday in the jazz/cabaret stakes. If Mary O'Brien knew all about Ella Fitzgerald, she would have also known Sara Vaughan, Carmen Macrae, Pearl Bailey, Abbey Lincoln and Betty Carter, the latter, as I write, still playing clubs such as New York's BLUE NOTE.

If white devils had been set free in Mary's head and heart, by the age of sixteen these were doing battle with some pretty potent black goddesses and she was being goaded by some pretty awesome black ghosts wailing their lamentations of hearts true and hearts broke.

Love and heartache for Mary O'Brien were already in her lost and found and she had not only the claim check but the key to the locker. If she knew, historically, how hard were the roads these blues singing women had travelled before her, it counted for nought. Mary knew she wanted to join them.

As Wilfred Mellers points out in his anthological ANGELS OF THE NIGHT, *"Gospel is communal music; the blues is solitary."* It was the making the solitary communally available which spawned the contemporary music industry and, though she didn't yet know it for sure, Mary O'Brien was in on the ground floor with more qualifications than she would ever need.

CHAPTER TWO

But how hard? How?

In the years between 1955 and 1958, between the ages of fifteen and nineteen, Mary started to take the prototype Dusty along with her, allowed her to tag along as she waited for the right moment to arrive for both of them. It must have been fun, at first, great fun, exploring the things that altered make-up and changed haircolour could achieve. She wasn't interested in making use of her natural attributes so the only answer was to make use of some unnatural ones.

For a time, Dusty was on her own at home as Dion, it would appear, was away in the army. Mary was the only child at home and as such, indulged by her parents as she explored the different avenues at her disposal in her pursuit of a singing career. She had already, at thirteen, cut her first record. DIY record booths were the rage. Dusty still has the recordings she made at age thirteen, thanks to her parents.

"... they were so supportive and I wanted to be so grown up. My father would come home in the rush hour and then get back on the tube at Ealing and go to the bowels of Belgravia to dig me out of some drinking club where I was singing for four hours for a guinea a night (One pound and one shilling i.e. One pound and five new pence). It was really nice of him but I gave him such a hard time ..."

In those days, way before she'd seen and been swayed by the inside workings of the recording studio, she just sang. Sang and sang.

"We used to get through a hundred songs in a night. Now, I wonder why I get laryngitis if I sing one. But it was okay then because no one was listening."

Assuming her personality to be as I have outlined, Dusty's frustrations must have been volcanic and her impatience almost uncontainable. How or through whom Mary got these singing gigs at Chelsea clubs like LE RASCAS, I know not, although she certainly sang with brother Dion a lot. At some of these venues, she found herself playing in front of big stars, film stars Michael Wilding and Rita Hayworth whom Dusty remembers specifically. Especially, she recalls Jack Lemmon to whom she is still grateful for taking time out to applaud her performance, but then Jack's a proper actor and knows what it's like. Mostly, people would talk through Dusty's act and pay her scant attention. People are like that. Leaves you seething for life and puts a very different light on singing for pleasure.

"I will sing under extreme ... If someone's got a gun to my head. I will sing for the hell of it with people who can really sing like Anne Murray and her family just sitting round a dining table - then I'll sing. Or if a song really affects me, I'll sing but I'm not ... I don't sing around the house or around the garden, you know, or anything like that - I never have ... Neither do I NEED to perform."

By educated guesswork, I also fancy that the Irish-Scottish girl from Ealing would not have been too enamoured with her close encounters with high society. I'm sure a handsome male singer with a dance band would have been fair game for predatory debutantes to fawn over but a not over-pretty, short-sighted female singer with a guitar they mistook for a banjo would probably have first been scorned, then spurned before ultimately being shown the servants' hall in which to change and the rear entrance through which to come and go. Though the debs' mothers tended to be at least kindlier, such high-handed off-handedness made Miss O'Brien very prickly. Many years later, the memory still irritated.

"... Y'know, doing deb balls and smart Mayfair clubs was

15

no real training. It was training to (pause) tune out idiots! (Mimics uppercrust accent) 'Oh, she's got her banjo'. My brother and I used to play the guitar. 'Sing che la la!' they always wanted you to sing something they'd heard on their ski-ing hols. But that was good training ...''

But Mary wasn't put off. She couldn't allow herself to be. She augmented her meagre income from singing by working in shops and department stores. She stuck with her singing even though it was on makeshift podia rather than proper theatrical stages. Although getting her to acknowledge her own linguistic abilities would be harder than pulling her teeth, a lot of Tom's linguistic skills had rubbed off on his gifted younger sister.

"I used to sing in all these different languages. Didn't know what I was singing about but I was an incredible mimic so I could sing in Turkish and I could sing in Spanish and I could sing in Portuguese with a Brazilian accent... To this day, I can't eat in a restaurant if there's a pianist or a guitarist because I feel so bad for them that I have to listen. So I can't possibly eat or if I eat I get indigestion. But to me it's the height of rudeness to turn my back on someone who's sweating it out there in the corner, or feeling degraded. It makes a miserable evening for me. It's awful. I mean, it's a rotten job, it really is a rotten job. But it's a way to make a buck."

Dusty acknowledges that she was spurred on by an inner conviction.

"I had this feeling and I don't know whether it was conceit or naivety but I knew it was going to be all right. Now I don't know how I knew it was going to be all right but I always knew ... way back when from when I decided I was going to become a singer. It was odd because we had no connections apart from the Gilbert and Sullivan touring great-grandparents in 1880 or something. But I just knew somehow it would all work out ..."

The moment that had been awaiting Mary finally arrived in 1958. By luck as much as by judgement - although isn't that just sometimes the way of it - Mary was reading a copy of THE STAGE, the weekly journal of the theatrical profession and in it saw an advertisement. The paper is always packed with adver-tisements, anything from chorus auditions for pantomime to magicians requiring assistants for shipboard cruising programmes. In 1958, there was more 'variety' than 'proper' theatre for in those days there were still variety theatres left to play in and not too many televisions.

"I answered an ad for 'Established sister act needs member' and I thought that would be ... (pause) ... a hoot. I needed stage experience as I had none ... I knew that if I joined something - an act - that actually worked, not in the sort of semi-amateur way but actually got booked by Tito Burns and things and actually went and did American air bases. Wah! That's ... If you can survive that, it's excellent training ..."

The act was the LANA SISTERS and it was run by Riss (Iris) Chantelle. The other existing member was Lynn Abrams and the vocal trio were partly managed by Eve Taylor, working out of the offices of the same company where Joe Collins worked, even then celebrated for fatherhood of his Hollywood starlet daughter Joan. Eve Taylor later went on to handle the careers of Adam Faith and Sandie Shaw. Whether Eve ever re-introduced herself to Dusty, history does not recall but had she done so, it would have been an interesting moment to have been a fly on the wall.

"We were rivals to the KAYE SISTERS. We hated THE MUDLARKS because THEY were successful. Not that we were unsuccessful. We didn't have hits but we had records. It taught me about lighting set-ups and microphones and television techniques because we used to appear on SIX FIVE SPECIAL and DRUMBEAT."

Mary was right to chose the LANA SISTERS to cut her teeth on, although it was the AVONS who had the hit with SEVEN LITTLE GIRLS SITTING IN THE BACK SEAT, a gruesome post-music hall concoction. I know because to my eternal shame, it was the first record I ever bought. Back seats and charabancs were integral to our growing up in the fifties and sixties for we went to school in them, went on Sunday school outings on them, went to choral competitions in them ... Oh!.

I'm glad Dusty wasn't in the AVONS. I don't think I would have felt the same about her had I known that. As a LANA SISTER, Mary first appeared costumed in a tulle skirt disguising an outfit of silver lame capri pants onstage at the Savoy cinema in Clacton. She tells the story of swearing in the dressing room whilst waiting to go on, refusing to go outside and turn round three times to atone for her oath and then paying the price of tripping and falling down the concrete stairs. When she finally flounced back the tulle skirt onstage it revealed her naked knees poking out of the split lame pants. Oh God, it's tough at the top.

After Dusty's having been accepted into the LANA SISTERS, the O'Brien household broke up for good. Both Mary and Dion flew the coop for Kay and OB moved to Brighton and grown-up life started in earnest for Mary. She first moved in with Lynn Abrams who lived with her parents in Hertford although later she moved into the West End where she lived in her own flat at the top of Baker Street, over, in those days, an ABC, gravy-with-everything restaurant.

From the very first, Mary was always to sing professionally under a name other than her given one. It was the start of a well-known but little-examined process of becoming someone other than yourself. 'Shan', as Riss Chantelle named Mary for CHANTELLE purposes, became a part of an act. Dusty still maintains that she has always thought of herself as part of a band, part of an orchestra. Her earlier duetting with Dion (Dieu-Donne, the God-given one, whom we shall henceforth call Tom) was now developed and Mary's obvious instinct for the construction of chords and harmony was developed. Dusty now insists that all this upbringing in harmony singing did not equip her naturally to sing lead and, as a LANA, she harmonised, Riss having the deeper voice. But it must have been a good apprenticeship.

"When THE SPRINGFIELDS came along, I actually was the only one that had set foot on a stage before. So in that way it was good tough training."

Pat Rhodes assured me that she would find out where the name THE SPRINGFIELDS came from. Thinking it was perhaps the name of an American town taken from some obscure bluesological source, Pat faithfully returned my enquiry with the answer: *"Because they used to go out and practise in the fields in spring."* Although clinging obstinately to my more esoteric reason, the birth of THE SPRINGFIELDS approached though I'd love to know where those fields were ... In the inner London suburbs?

Tom was the creative force and guiding influence behind THE SPRINGFIELDS. He had not graduated from school to university but had worked in the City. His linguistic ability was as catholic as his upbringing had been Cathlolic. He spoke or a least understood several languages and was, according to John Altham, fluent in Russian to the extent that, from those cold war days, the story has come down that he was even involved with MI5! We know he translated and adapted many European and South American songs and was greatly influenced by ethnic folk sources from all over the world. Tim Feild had travelled extensively and was obviously a soulmate of Tom's as far as embracing ethnic material was concerned. In those sunny spring fields, it seems inconceivable that Tom did not envision Dusty singing lead. He must have done and, like the good little sister, when big brother taught, Dusty indented, the London apprentice.

"... my brother was the ideas man. It certainly didn't come through me ... He was good at that. He would adapt Russian folksongs and things and make commercial songs out of them."

When asked whether THE SPRINGFIELDS consciously bore any similarity to anyone else from the arty, black-mohair-sweater and existentialist-leggings, seriously-intellectual groups and folk artists of the time, Dusty didn't hesitate:

"No! None whatsoever. (We were) absolutely cheerful as hell ... In actual fact, we weren't, basically, but we appeared to be and we didn't sing very in tune but we sang quite loudly and there was just a niche there for us at that time where we could do sort of things like WIMOWEH and ... I cracked up, I saw a clip not so long ago of THE SPRINGFIELDS doing (sings snatch of WIMOWEH) and I announced it. I'd obviously been to the Sylvia Peters school of announcing 'cos I went, (effects 'posh' voice), 'That was a Zulu Tune'. I don't believe I said that! And I still had my red hair, the hair I was born with which was, being Irish-Scottish, was bright red ... So, we were able to do semi-country, we were very affected by people like THE WEAVERS who were an American Folk Group ... But it was ... we managed to make sort of a record that sounded semi-country which was an enormous hit in The States so they grabbed us off there thinking we were a country group and we weren't remotely. I mean they were writing songs in the morning and

expecting us to sing them in the afternoon. It took us three weeks to rehearse one verse for some things so it was a pretty frightening experience.. No we just sang whatever ... No, my brother had a lot to do with it but somewhere along the way I sensed that we were all in it as a means to an end. It served us very well and when we split up it was, not as some people viewed it, my going off on my own. I mean, my brother had 'had it' (and) that he wrote some very successful things thereafter for THE SEEKERS and things which sort of followed on from THE SPRINGFIELDS very well for him. We were all in it sort of to gain experience and try to enjoy it as much as we could."

The Dusty who speaks in interviews at the time like the one above, bears little relation to her later incarnation as a solo performer. Speaking as she was as part of a group, as one of a trio, her reported words are gentler, more grounded. Of the nature of THE SPRINGFIELDS she says in 1961 (although the heavy hand of the Sylvia Peters school of journalism wreaks havoc with Dusty's original pearls):

"We're not what you might call authentic folk singers. Ours is a slightly commercial approach to folk music because in this way we hope to win the acceptance of the public as a whole and not just a minority section ... Our individual tastes in music are very varied. Brother Tom is a real folk music enthusiast. Tim is mad about Latin American music and my personal taste ranges from jazz and rhythm-n-blues to Latin music. Apart from classical music, folk music is the one thing we all agree on. Also, since there are very few folk groups on the pop scene, the adoption of a folksy-spiritual style has enabled us to create a rather distinctive and easily recognisable sound ... But we do enjoy singing rock 'n' roll and our next single in the New Year will be a much more beaty item. It'll be very different from our previous discs."

How I love that word 'beaty'!

Basically what she's saying is that to work in a group, compromise is usually the order of the day. I find the psychology of association quite fascinating in the context of the music industry. It seems endlessly interesting to me, the process by which two, three or four people decide it worthwhile to sacrifice hours of hardwork to dedicated practice and rehearsal and, thereafter, several years of a precious life committing to mutual association only to find that the reasons why you thought you liked your partners sufficiently to risk all have turned into the very reasons why you just can't bear to remain another minute in their company. Having witnessed them first hand in two serious management companies, the politics which go on behind the scenes even in the appointment or removal of even of a novice roadie put Machiavelli's mediaeval tactics in the creation of popes and princes in the shade.

Tim Feild ultimately removed himself and Tom and Dusty auditioned. Mike Hurst had Variety in his blood. His mother, Flavia Pickworth ran a children's troupe and Mike had grown up in the business. He was tall, good-looking and professional. He replaced Tim Feild but on his own admission, although he sang with Tom and Dusty, he was never integral to policy, which seems to have been basically Tom's, angled by Dusty. Tom is supposed not to have liked performing, preferring songwriting and Dusty, in those days, was willing to go with performance as long as she could have her own career on her own terms. "She was a tough lady," Mike Hurst avers.

Basic policy was that they would see where THE SPRINGFIELDS led and go with it. However, even if the act became entirely successful, a determination would take place after three years. The policy seems to have been adhered to because, according to Pat Rhodes, Dusty has confirmed that the material for her first singles and album had been recorded before THE SPRINGFIELDS officially split up.

There was a masterplan.

"It seems like we were being set up without my really having anything to do with it apart from being fairly calculating."

From photographs taken of Dusty sandwiched between Tom and Tim, THE SPRINGFIELDS days seem to have been happy.

"We were pseudo-everything," Dusty said recently, pressed to attribute influences, "and we knew it. I mean, we just jumped up and down a lot and were cheerful which was ... there was a niche somewhere for cheerful people and we were terribly out of tune. We just sang very fast and very cheerfully and at the time

it was ... like the Kingston trio were happening and there wasn't really a British version of ... they were all men."

Being 'merely' Tom's sister, it seems that Dusty began her career not being exactly pampered. It seems from the following comment that it was assumed that she, willy nilly, because she was a girl, could therefore be allotted the maternal, 'looking after' role:

"... I mean, we'd change trains in Crewe and the boys would leave their mikes on the station and their guitars and go off and have a cheese sandwich whereas I would sit with the mikes and guitars because I knew someone was going to steal them and then we wouldn't be able to play in wherever we were going to play - Galashiels or something. And I'd say, 'But if they were stolen, we wouldn't have been able to do the show' and they'd say, 'Great!'."

Assumed to be responsible and assuming responsibility is a habit that establishes itself in the eyes of others faster than Japanese knotweed in an English country garden. Not a bad plant in itself, knotweed unfortunately prevents anything else from growing. Being responsible without having the power is a nasty rut to slip into. Very hard to get out of and very galling, especially if the rut goes on for miles ... and miles. Being in that position always teaches you, not malignly but nevertheless efficiently, not to trust others, only to trust yourself.

"We just did record after record after record and it worked. I mean, that was the hard work but I never had to struggle to get there although that doesn't negate all the struggling we did catching the all-night bus in Oxford Street after appearing at Churchill's in Bond Street and getting off at Ealing Broadway and walking two miles home in thick fog. Those were the struggling days."

This 'Good Companions' sort of existence, travelling from booking to booking, even when the hits had started coming, was par for the course in those early sixties.

"... we did the ballrooms and they were always in the middle of a field somewhere, right? And they started very late which was fine with me. What I loved about it was that no matter what the hour was, they'd open up the shops for you afterwards

or give you a meal. You know, the hotel kitchen would open up for you and give you steak and mash ..."

There was no option to these schedules. Every 'hit parade'- successful act did it because the business was still set up to deal with acts, acts as they had existed for years on the music hall and, as it was commuted, the variety circuits. The life bred its own stresses and strains and made for strange bedfellows. Lately, Dusty has even gone so far as to say:

"We (THE SPRINGFIELDS) weren't even friendly with each other, let alone to the world. But it was a means to an end for all of us. I was the worrier and still am. I was the one that always wanted to get it right and that's the way I continue to be ... Conscientious to the end. I've always wanted to get it right. That's how I was in school. A bit thick but extremely conscientious."

Though Tom made musical policy, the everyday affairs of THE SPRINGFIELDS were handled by Emlyn Griffiths, essentially a 'booker' of acts. Pat Rhodes knew him well. She came , to work for him having started at Kavanagh, the literary agents, at the suggestion of a friend. Though being interviewed for the job of receptionist/telephonist which she got, Pat also taught herself to type and made herself generally indispensable. She remembers Emlyn, suave and beautifully dressed, sporting a monocle. He would spend a lot of time out of the office, often sipping his pink gins at QUAGLINO'S in London's St. James's, the entertainment club and lounge off Jermyn Street. Many of the artists Emlyn represented would be booked there and he was as famous as they. However, he was one of a large number of theatrical executives whose careers would soon be past. Though charming and wonderful company, he would never make the transition into the new world which the growth of pop music opened up.

Management was not a factor at work in Dusty's early career. If anyone did it, the performers 'managed' themselves, viz. Riss with THE LANA SISTERS and Tom with THE SPRINGFIELDS. In those days, record companies made no contribution to their artists' touring and performing expenses and neither did the song publishers whose royalties were effectively earned by the singers who, unpaid in that respect, merely sang the songs ...

Artists' agents in those days wouldn't have thought of asking for a bite of the publishing apple on behalf of their workhorse clients. Percentage points on recording contracts were minimal and obligations onerously loaded in the artists' direction; agents either didn't understand or were fearful of pressing record companies too hard and lawyers yet hadn't sniffed the bigger bucks waiting at the edges of the vinyl perimeter. Augmenting performance sounds so that the concert audiences heard, live, what at least approximated to the recorded sound was never paid for by record companies. The artists in those days footed all their own bills other than the actual studio and session expenses.

Dusty grew up with that state of affairs being the norm. She developed with no history of artists' management as a scientific business operation integral to a star's being a star and remaining so. What the artists were left with was theirs for others to con out of them.

Dusty was also developing confused about her musical direction. Knowing so much and being able to do most things, she had yet to find what really turned her on, the heat that popped her artistic corn.

"Bunny Lewis, who was a manager - used to manage THE MUDLARKS way back - had two criticisms of me. He said: 'A) you'll never make it because you're too intelligent and B) you'll never make it 'cos you can't make up your mind what you want to sing ... You have to make up your mind what you want to sing."

One thing is certain, when Dusty did come to choose, it certainly wasn't the obvious. Though she might now assert that she had grown up NOT being the one outfront, trained to take second place, Dusty's hitherto unfocused and wide-ranging musicality finally shuddered into focus when THE SPRINGFIELDS' folk-influenced music, notably SILVER THREADS AND GOLDEN NEEDLES, led them to heed Shelby Singleton's encouragement and to record FOLKSONGS FROM THE HILLS in Nashville, Tennessee, USA.

"I loved that song! It was really great. It was a really good record. It was a complete fluke, a complete and utter fluke. We

weren't country singers but it was the whole thing that led Nashville to think that we were country singers."

For a girl brought up on everything American, the trip must have been almost an apotheosis. Dusty sets the scene talking to Mike Hellicar in 1962:

"Our trip to Nashville changed everything for us. There's no doubt it channelled us into doing country and western music without us knowing it. These days we seem to be doing all country and western music ... (Of their first BBC audition) A producer (BBC) told us: 'You must make up your minds to be either a folk group or a pop group if you're going to be any success at all.' But of course we fall between the two. One of the difficulties of being THE SPRINGFIELDS is that there is lots of material we would like to sing but we must be careful not to steer into an arty or poppy category. You see we haven't enough class for a folk concert and not enough pop background for a rock concert ... Actually we don't set out to make our singles the genuine country and western article for it just wouldn't go down. We prefer to do the rowdy commercial country music that record buyers prefer."

You can almost hear Dusty 'acting' being what she thought was a country and western singer. An excellent mimic as we know, she invests her delivery and pronunciation with an extra coating of hillbilly twang. Was she sending the stuff up? Tom hotly defended his sister.

In 1989, she admitted to Q Magazine:

"We weren't at all comfortable with that happy, breezy music. And I was just doing it to get famous - I was a fairly calculating bastard."

Being pigeon-holed, hoist forever by your very own petard, boxed in by other people's perceptions ... That certainly wasn't what Dusty was after. Despite the folksy mantle she allowed it to be presumed she was wearing after Nashville, the experience was a turning point for her both on an artistic and professional count, to say nothing of the eye-opener it was on the business front.

"Only when I first went to the States and heard black music - black pop music - that I discovered ... THAT was the music I wanted to hear."

*"The biggest high I can think of was the first time I heard
DON'T MAKE ME OVER by Dionne Warwick. I was in Nashville.
(The Capital Motor Inn) It was about 1962 and I had to sit down
very suddenly because I thought: 'That's what I want to do. It
changed my life. I thought: 'That's ... that's changing music.'
Nobody can sing Bacharach and David music like her. Nobody.
Because it's gossamer. Total gossamer ... But the songs were
there in the first place. But I think Bacaharach changed - and
Hal David at the time - changed the course of pop music
probably more than anyone else despite ... more than the
Beatles, more than anything but it was more subtle. It wasn't
like: 'Look, we're changing music.' But they just went about
their business and changed it."*

*"... the construction was so sophisticated, he was using
time signatures no one had used in pop music and so I sat down
suddenly. I thought I'd died and gone to heaven! I'm not a
musician per se. I don't read but I knew that I hadn't heard that
before and in fact in pop music, it hadn't been done before ... and
Cissie Houston's voice on the top there ... Those were incredible
sounds."*

More succinctly she, lately, has explained:

*"I knew I wanted to do something but I didn't know what
it was until I heard it. Actually, I'd first heard it briefly in New
York. We had a stopover in New York (en route for Nashville) -
my first time (there) ever and I was going past a record shop and
I heard TELL HIM by THE EXCITERS blaring out, late night."*

Knowing that there was something else out there and
being very conscious that she wasn't doing it was frustrating.
Nashville recording techniques were also a million miles away
from what she was used to.

*"... it was disastrous for us because everyone was very
nice to us but, you know, they didn't realise it took us three weeks
to rehearse one verse and in Nashville at that time, you know,
they'd write the song in the morning and you'd go in and start
recording it in the afternoon. And they were writing the music
parts on the balcony and throwing down the violin part as
you're singing so the stress of that ... we were hopeless and we
just didn't work. They were still very nice to us ... though we
weren't country singers. It was a shock to them to discover that.*

Hey ... we were up for it ... we just didn't know how to work that quickly and stylistically. I don't know what we were but we weren't that ... Well, you can imagine what it must have been like for me. I always want to get everything right. I couldn't possibly. I sort of blocked most of it. All I remember is going to these peoples' houses, you know, going to their dens - they always had dens! And everything was kind of flock wallpaper and curlicues. They tell me it's changed ..."

I must have said this a million times before but in case anyone's missed the point about America, it's this. America empowers. It makes you FEEL you can BE and DO anything. The process works potently on Americans themselves. It works double on impressionable young Europeans. Whilst in Nashville, Dusty was made aware of the potential of those fifty wonderful states:

"We went along to see a local DJ 'biggie' called Ralph Emery at the (Radio) station that produces The Grand Ole Opry. Ralph has a nationwide programme and we just sat down and talked to him over the air for about fifteen minutes. It was a marvellous experience. The informality of it all and yet the knowledge that millions of people all over the States are listening to you."

The 'it's-laid-back-but-it-gets-done' nature of Uncle Sam seduced and perplexed Dusty by turns for decades.

The Nashville album in a way vindicated Dusty's earlier pronouncements about being boxed in. THE SPRINGFIELDS were veering towards the esoteric, away from pop. I have no doubt that the break-up of THE SPRINGFIELDS, despite the way Mike Hurst has loyally proclaimed the spontaneity of it, was entirely calculated. Dusty says so, between the lines in 1963, to John Hunt:

"Everybody tells us we're mad ... Well, we always have been mad. It's (the break-up) a big chance and we're taking it ... It's better to take this terrific gamble while we are at the top rather than when we are on the way down."

Tom vindicated her. He told Pete Goodman:

"Since the news broke, I'm more than happy to say that we've all had some excellent offers. Dusty for instance had engagements lined up for her that she'd never have thought

possible. All right, so she's my sister but I think she's going to be one of the biggest names in the business."

I love 'engagements'... Princess Margaret always has engagements! And I'm very glad Dusty had them too. She claimed that she left THE SPRINGFIELDS with less than £100 and a lot of white shirts. That's some theatrical dowry!

Ivor Raymonde, later to conveniently go on to be a very big noise in BBC Radio who would play Dusty's records to bits, was already arranging music for THE SPRINGFIELDS and he had already recorded THAT song with Dusty. Johnny Franz was their recording manager and obviously became Dusty's. New recording contracts were easily available to Dusty at Phillips from Fontana. The agency agreement with Emlyn Griffiths was determined by the decision of Tom and Dusty to disband the group although Dusty was quick to retain Pat Rhodes whose efficiency and loyalty had become invaluable to Dusty. What was left behind was left behind as Dusty crossed the stepping stones to the solo unknown.

But 'the buzz' as she has called it, was deafening. Solo, she had already appeared on JUKE BOX JURY and on a television special entitled HERE COME THE GIRLS. *"Suddenly Dusty Springfield is emerging as an interesting personality,"* the NME wrote with characteristic brillo and enthusiasm in 1963.

"THE SPRINGFIELDS finished, officially, at the London Palladium but I think there were a couple more things we had to do. It wasn't exactly difficult. I was singing solo actually in the last days of THE SPRINGFIELDS and oddly enough I came second in an NME poll for solo singers when I was still with the THE SPRINGFIELDS. I ONLY WANT TO BE WITH YOU was recorded before THE SPRINGFIELDS were finished and actually it took three weeks to go from being a SPRINGFIELD to being a solo ..."

Pondering the past more analytically, Dusty explained:

"There are psychological moments for things and I had enough intuition to know. The buzz ... There WAS a buzz. I knew that when I did solo things and the audience reaction to me. It just made it quite clear that's what I should do."

One thing Dusty really left behind, for several years, was, finally, Mary O'Brien who had been transformed via her child-

hood nickname 'Dusty' via Mary Springfield to Dusty Springfield and Dusty Springfield was going to find herself far too
busy over the next six years to pay much attention to poor
languishing Mary.

CHAPTER THREE

She only wants
to be with... you!!

"I care what I look like," Quentin Crisp said, *"because it's the means of presenting to the world the way I am. The way I look is the way I think I am."*

Yes, folks. It's that easy.

All mothers think their daughters are beautiful and all daughters want to be beautiful. If she's not, you make her beautiful. You make her look like what you want her to look like, what your daughter thinks she is. If Kay O'Brien had been Dr. Frankenstein and Mary was Igor, the monster they were working on underwent many, many transplants, implants and road tests before it finally flowered in the shape and form of their piece de resistance, Miss Dusty Springfield.

Mary willingly abandoned herself to be enfolded by the arms of her creation as would any self-respecting teenage girl given the same opportunity. Instead of an image of self-perfection achieved in the heart-shaped mirror, on the white, frilled kidney-shaped dressing table, an image designed to last just for a few hours on a Saturday night, the image and edifice of Dusty Springfield was designed to be immutable, a temple, a haven, an indestructible bastion, to last not only through the rest of the following week but for the foreseeable forever. A lifetime.

So, at last, ladies and gentlemen, would you welcome ... Miss ... Dusty ... Springfield!

And there she was.

The 'Miss' would never become a 'Mrs', the Springfield would never change to Penkowski or Fish or Watanabe. That there could have been a Mister Dusty Springfield was entirely conceivable; a nice self-effacing consort, like Prince Philip, content to walk two paces behind the incandescent supernova that was Miz' Dusty Springfield. Dusty Springfield had been designed for, and by, two eternal, patient and very professional fans. Kay and Mary O'Brien.

In 1968, Dusty gave one version of what it's like to be two people and yet to be neither of them. Her words make for an insupportable contradiction and an unviable psychological existence on a long term basis and they scream out as such. Such a fate, truly, is the price of fame and it seems that it must be for every actor and singer as well as a lot of writers seem to go in for re-inventing themselves, creating the person they've always wanted to be, the person they need to be to do whatever it is they do. It is one of those strange rituals of western culture. These words of Dusty's could have been spoken by anyone of a million peers.

"I feel like two separate people. I was coming here tonight and I saw my name up in lights. People say: It must give you a kick seeing your name up there', but it doesn't ... It doesn't give me a thrill. Not because I'm ungrateful ... it's just that it seems like a separate person. When I hear my name announced, it also feels to me like it's someone else."

Is it guilt that makes people want to change their names? Is it self-loathing which drives people to want to escape their original selves so desperately, to swap their psyche for a mere perception of a personality which is by nature void, utterly insubstantial and yet incapable of independent existence without the fundamental origin of the self that has been so cruelly eschewed? Is it so ludicrous and embarrassing to stand up and sing out as Reginald Dwight or Miss Ciccone? Is this changing name business a latent phenomenon which could make Elton Johns and Madonnas of us all? Has anyone ever created both the alter ego and the matching carapace to house the soft-shelled creature? It all ends up as a kind of auto-cannibalism.

It's highly indigestible stuff but we go on doing it. Society decrees that half the western world's population upon entering the state of marriage change their names. So, yes ... It probably is latent, for who but slaves would have done the work of women for centuries without having changed themselves by changing their names and making that slavery bearable? The symbol of a man, his name, consumes a woman. And it's legal. The only way to make the whole mess of pottage palatable at all is to wrap it all up with the ribbons of romantic love. Hearts and flowers. Tally ho. Chocs and away ...

Drifting further into irony, it is odd that our very youth makes many of us naturally bad pupils. We listen, but we rarely learn and by the time we have, the lessons of time are useless. It's all the wrong way round, really. Why do we know in our middle age what we didn't know when we needed to know it when we were young ... Ah, what the heck!

But, to return to our girl. Freeze your frames on the night before I ONLY WANT TO BE WITH YOU was first played to the British public over the radio airwaves. Let's take a little stock, here.

Beneath the slap, the dye-job and the hairpieces, there's this girl, a shortish girl, short-sighted, short legs, Irish-Scottish with red hair, few qualifications. She feels ineffective, inadequate, compromised and confused and guilty. From her publicly-made self-pronouncements, she didn't like herself too much. I don't blame this girl in the slightest because this girl, however much she both doubted and denied it, was also very, very intelligent. What Mary saw in the mirror was the truth. I should capitalise that sentence because it's very, very important.

The truth is very important to men and women like Dusty for unless you know the truth, feel it as a burning issue, you cannot lie; you have no need to lie. Without either burning truth or practised lies you just have ... ordinariness. Nothing. No perspective. Endlessness. Nothing burns, not even does anything smoulder or sputter and it is, therefore, never extinguished ... The Dustys of this world HAVE to get up and DO something for if they don't, the alternative is unthinkable. You see, stretching out before you, a slow, agonisingly slow, spiritual death.

Dusty had developed emotional sensitivity as keen as radar; she also knew she was different, that she didn't feel the same way about life, the future, boys, babies as the majority of her peers. It's a strange limbo to have to swim around in, checking the edges, knowing the frontiers, exploring the entrances and exits. Girls of that age know what they SHOULD do; they don't know what they can do if they choose not to do as they SHOULD. Dusty, a more than averagely sensitised young woman, could anticipate hurt and could contemplate being either trapped or left out and she avoided both by withdrawing and ducking under the fence into fantasy, a world of her own creation.

But once you choose not to do what you SHOULD, you have proverbially either to shit or get off the pot. You have to get out and get on or else ... Or else forget it; take the SHOULD option and stay where you are and brazen life out.

Dusty never had to feel guilty, at least about sloth or lack of dynamism although she has often proclaimed her laziness. She had a lot of people on her side, people who didn't want her life to be like theirs. Dusty unconsciously became a dream merchant, destined to travel the wish roads of other people's lives, bearing their cargoes of escapism which they could not afford to carry, doing what they would and could never do because of their indenture to their lives of SHOULD.

Thus buoyed up, Dusty was therefore able to slambition her way through teenage, not needing to do any of the boyfriend/ dance hall/coffee bar/youth club things that others were doing to get themselves married. This girl knew she wasn't going to be snapped up and she knew she didn't want to be. Kay had married late. There was always that option to fall back on but Kay more than anything wanted Mary to succeed, to not fall into the maw of the marriage machine.

In those days, choices for women were very, very limited. Very, very few would ever get to be able to say NO. It's caused a whole heap of trouble. Mary didn't have to choose. She knew it wasn't going to happen for her. Instead, there was something much better than the inevitable drudgery, the inevitable children. No need for lying and deceit and dissembling. As Miss ... Dusty ... Springfield she wouldn't need to, didn't have to. Instead ...

The 'instead' for Mary was the glamour conspiracy with Dusty Springfield. The trouble, (for none of us escapes our share), with conspiracies is that they have to be controlled and they have to be acknowledged and mutually fed. The covert HAS to succour the conspiracy and vice-versa and their roles must NEVER be blurred. Out of control, conspiracies cease to function profitably and, unacknowledged they negate their mutual reality. The conspiracy has to have as much reality as the covert and, if it assumes a shape, must inhabit a doppelganger as strong as the original. Each therefore has to tell the other the truth. Tell a lie, perpetuate a lie, believe a lie and both creations are in dead, dead shtuck for both will surely be found out. If, as Pat Rhodes confirmed to me, the overlap between the two characters in the Mary/Dusty constellation is too confusing for most people to deal with, what on earth is it like for their common soul?

Dusty was twenty four when she went solo. That's some age to still feel insecure. Most people even if they could acknowledge the insecurity, couldn't afford it. She must have taken pleasure in the way her new persona was being perceived as THE SPRINGFIELDS career blossomed: *'Attractive Mary Springfield'*, *'glamourous red-head'* and, finally, *'vivacious blonde'* was how various critics and, respectively, Don Short described her in 1963.

Dusty was obviously unsatisfied. Perhaps she was drawn to amplifying her physical image in the same way she wanted to mould the way she sounded?

"I've always wanted to emulate people who have big voices and people always think that I have a big voice but I don't. It sounds like that, maybe, on record but actually I don't. But that's what I wanted to sound like."

"... the need to get rid of the person that you were, the need ... it does take talent to realise that person's a no-hoper, I mean, the next layer of talent is to get rid of her and try and become this other person and if you invent the person as I did in a different way - and many people have - then that person (the original) really is useless. Until, as you get older, you start to realise that person has some value ..."

Having an image of your career likened to Peggy Lee's and sounding also like Ella Fitzgerald, Dusty's resulting glamourous Hollywood blonde coiffure, with the complementary, impossibly exaggerated maquillage (for which she ought to have won the Queen's Award to the cosmetic industry) were not over-the-top at all. Au contraire, it seemed that with unerring taste, Dusty Springfield's image fitted the bill her waiting public wanted. The blonde female singer featured with the dance band had become an institution throughout the world. Frances Langford with Glenn Miller, Kathy Kirby still doing it with Ambrose, Doris Day had done it for years. Blondes were certainly thought to have more fun.

"So, just one day my brother tells me, I just went to Harrods, bought a black sheath dress, a string of pearls, put my hair up into a chignon and was a different person. That's what I'm told ..."

But what a millstone!

Unfreeze the frame. Let the documentary roll.

Dusty is putting on her make-up. It takes her hours. Like Dolly Parton whom she preceded, like many other glamour blondes, from 1963 onwards Dusty will take forever to apply her face, to turn Mary O'Brien into Dusty Springfield. Dusty Springfield hates being seen without the slap on. Mary O'Brien prefers lounging about 'au naturel'.

Sisters, sisters ... were there never more devoted sisters?

"The one time I was too tired to do all that, you know, to put the make-up on ... no matter what time we got back from the night before, I still got up in the morning and did all that. Me and my behive on the (tour) 'bus, eight o'clock in the morning, Madame Tussaud's. I'll never forget it. Sitting bolt upright. The one time I was too tired to do it, we got off the 'bus somewhere like Exeter, maybe Bristol, the 'bus pulled up backstage and I had a scarf on and I hadn't done my make-up properly and I heard two people say, 'Oooh, she doesn't look good, does she?' I never did it again.

But I always remember Joan Crawford used to never leave the studio with her make-up on from the set. She would always go to the dressing room, take it off, put a face on, a public Joan Crawford face because fans would stop the car at the gate, the studio gate ... She'd make that effort every day and in the morning too. It must have been very wearying."

At that moment, Dusty remembers JUST how wearying it was.

"That WAS wearying, by the way, putting on all that stuff. I mean, the boys would pour onto the 'bus with hangovers and all that and we couldn't get away with that ... I have to spend an inordinate amount of time becoming that person. It takes longer and longer, actually. That's why I probably would never have made a very good actress because it takes me so long to become Dusty Springfield that if I had to become another person on top of it, it'd be truly exhausting ... It feels odd, because I did invent her. I invented me ... It's not a split personality per se but I'm a very, very private person and the Mary O'Brien part ... you know, the fat convent schoolchild that suddenly became someone else but is still there, the person that I have to smash down and say: 'No! you're not too shy to do it, you're not, you ARE good enough.' And there's till my mother's voice saying: 'Sing up, Mary', because she's always ... I think that's the critic. The critic says that it's never good enough and I was trying to please my mum. I used to think Mary was hopeless and useless and everything else and too vulnerable, too this and too that and so I hid behind the Dusty Springfield thing."

It was not as if the disaster stories were not well-known. Marilyn Monroe, Jennifer Jones ... Hollywood stars were living and dying by the route Dusty was taking. But Dusty was buying into the fantasy, taking out stock in glamour as though she was taking out a lifetime subscription to American Express. There was no downside. It would do nicely.

"It's marvellous to be popular but foolish to think it will last," she is famously quoted as saying in 1963 when I ONLY WANT TO BE WITH YOU reached number eighteen in the UK chart by the twenty-first of November. From there it climbed to number 4 and spent thirteen weeks on the chart.

"I was just very lucky ... I didn't exactly have to claw my way to the top ... I don't know whether it's innate conceit or stupidity or genuine information about myself that led me to believe that it would all work out. I had no idea."

CHAPTER FOUR

Hope and fancy

Dusty's follow-up single, STAY AWHILE, was issued in February 1964 and her first album, A GIRL CALLED DUSTY was released in April. Its launch was followed by I JUST DON'T KNOW WHAT TO DO WITH MYSELF in June. Neither single was included on the album. In those days, you never did. Singles were NEVER on albums and to do so was considered bad form, not giving value for money for an artist to earn twice on the same work. Now? Shucks.

Dusty's sixties singles were immensely contemporary. It was thought so at the time and it is obviously and unarguably so listening to them almost thirty years on. Their style and substance fell in step seamlessly with the progressive march of American influenced pop music, a blend of treble and top sprayed rather like a jet of graffiti on a wall of sound. Very alive ... Like you're there. Very happening.

It must not be forgotten that there were no rules as far as making records were concerned in those days. It was people like Dusty who wrote what passed for rules with pens begged borrowed or stolen from their peers. So little had gone before which they could use as yardsticks. There was so little history. There was no other generation.

There was also no point in having rules as such. By the mid-sixties, technology began to change so rapidly that state-of-the-art recording facilities remained state-of-the-art for no longer than six months.

Everybody knows - and if they don't, they should - that Dusty was ultimately her own producer and before confirming that, I'd like to examine what it is exactly that a record producer does. I fear I've known some in my time who've earned a very easy percentage and a totally undeserved career on the back of, basically, someone else's recipe. Take equal proportions of studio time and session musicians and mix thoroughly with a commissioned arrangement. Add echo and bake, according to budget, for about two sessions, that's about five hundred pounds on the 1963 scale, perhaps a little more depending on the age of the century. Oh! When it's cooked, add a sprinkling of vocal, for the colour. Turn out onto black vinyl, wrap in fancy but not extravagant paper envelopes and sell. They'll love it.

This wasn't for Dusty. She'd heard what she wanted to do, knew it in her head, had spent years, like Glen Miller, looking for 'that sound'. Having found it, she was determined not to settle for second best.

Achievement is a very simple equation, really. Power plus Responsibility equals Control. $P + R = C$. Much more germane to the human condition than Einstein's $E = MC$ squared.

To have control, you must have the power to effect the responsibility you feel. Dusty has always keenly felt the need to be in control. Subsequent chapters will deal with her fiercely independent stances on every aspect of her career. Perhaps she adhered to these stances too vehemently at the time. I prefer to believe that perhaps she didn't. Control is a very volatile commodity. Once you begin to share it, once you give even an inch or an ounce away, it's awfully hard to get it back into the bottle. And there's never enough money in the world to buy back lost integrity.

This chapter was going to be just about work. It must also be about gender for when I say that Dusty suffered from the Margaret Thatcher syndrome, I am comparing neither to neither but merely illustrating a point. Margaret Thatcher was widely thought 'strident' and 'bossy' whereas, it has been suspected, that a male equivalent may have been perceived instead as 'dynamic' and 'dominant'. Dusty, being a woman ... Well, it just wasn't very nice, was it? I mean, she was only a slip of a girl ... You can almost hear the rumbling round the tea urn as the men waited for the uppity bitch to fall flat on her arse.

"... I was asking musicians to play sounds they'd never heard before. For instance, Motown hadn't released any records in Britain but I'd heard them on tour in the States. I wanted to use those influences in a country where they were still playing stand-up bass and the only black music they knew about was jazz. So, I would scowl a lot. They knew what I wanted but the last person they were going to take it from was a beehived bird."

But, according to Billy Wilder, as Valentino said to Norma Desmond: 'It takes tiles to tango properly ...' Dusty HAD to do it properly too.

"By then I was on to wanting to cop Phil Spector's sounds and I knew that I could. I wanted to be THE CRYSTALS and Darlene Love and knew that there was going to be a space for that in this country because it hadn't hit here and I definitely knew that that wall of sound thing could be adapted for England and I was the one to do it ..."

Getting what she wanted meant getting it yesterday. There was no time for gentle research and genteel experiment. Little by little by little by little was never anywhere in it.

"... I drove the musicians crazy, drove the engineer crazy but I got a pretty good approximation. I knew that's what I wanted to do. I knew that it could work. I've no idea how I knew, but I did ... But remember, I had an extremely indulgent recording manager who would let me do it. I mean, Johnny (Franz) was a sweetheart. He'd read popular mechanics and I'd go in and tell Johnny what to do but he knew that I knew what I was talking about and he knew he didn't. Now, a lot of people would say - would still want to even though they didn't know - but, I tell you, HE KNEW when someone was playing something wrong. Like the sax. He had perfect pitch so he would say: 'That should be a B not a B flat,' which I couldn't do. I could only sing it. I'd have to take the chord apart and that takes a very long time to explain to a musician. If someone in there says; 'It should be a B natural', it's so much quicker. So ... He (Johnny) was a real gent, no longer with us, but somehow he knew that I knew what I was doing and on that level, he didn't ..."

It still amazes me to consider that Dusty has never learned to read music. Or, so she says. She maintains, quite truthfully, that she had very bad eyesight which was compensated by her incredible hearing! So maybe she doesn't read music like she'd read a novel. But 'Every Good Boy Deserves Favour'. Even I know about that!

A lot of record companies had their own studios. In fact, they all did. 'Indies' were unheard of. There were only four British record companies; several labels, but all divisions of the larger parents. Dusty's was Phillips/Pye having come from Fontana, a subdivision, whilst she was with THE SPRINGFIELDS.

"Marble Arch was hard because there were only four tracks and so the internal balance on any one track ... you were stuck with. You'd end up with some maniac putting a bass on the same track as the strings and by then, you know ... and all I did was hang over - God bless Peter Oliff who was the engineer at Phillips at the time - the control board and turn the reverb knob up so that the drums sounded as though the household cavalry had just gone past and any mistakes were buried ... that gave it bigness. When in doubt, turn the echo knob up! Phillips was an extremely dead studio and to this day I can't stand it. It sounded as though someone had turned down the treble on everything and it was essential to get an edge on things. I couldn't get an edge. I don't have an 'edgy' voice and, then, didn't know about EQ-ing. The whole thing was like carpet and sound baffles and things I can't stand. There was no ambience and it was like singing in a padded cell and, you know, I'd land up feeling like I was IN a padded cell. I had to get out of there!"

There was no upping and offing and 'See you in Montserrat' or 'You can see Lake Geneva from the window'. Artists didn't have that kind of say or sway in those days. That was what recording managers were really for, to ensure that budgets and schedules were STRICTLY adhered to. Artists were seen as potentially unruly and anarchic schoolchildren by their record companies. Dusty had to record where she was put.

"Probably in the ladies loo at Phillips at two or three in the morning ... because the sound in the corridor was right. And no one was doing that and so I was viewed with a mixture of fear and ... there's a word for it ... Behind my back they were

probably stabbing me furiously and I'm not being paranoid because I know it's the truth ... Then, you know, they used to play track to speakers. The mike was dead on the back so you had to have them really low. Well, I have to have them on the threshold of pain, the headphones on the threshold of pain, for me even to utter a note. That's where I get my courage from - Sheer decibel level ... So I was always working within tremendous restrictive conditions and just dying to bust out of it by anyway I could and the more hits I had the more indulgent they became ... to that point where I DID end up in the ladies' loo because that's where it was live ... The end of the corridor was CLOSE MY EYES AND COUNT TO TEN."

I suppose the only people who could have understood what it was that Dusty was after in the studio were people like her who had already travelled to America. Very few Brits had. Those were only JUST the days of the Boeing 707. 747's were a thing of the future. It was cheaper to travel third class on a transatlantic Queen than to fly. The sea crossing took five days. The star musicians in the hit bands who were Dusty's peers had certainly crossed the Atlantic but they were too engrossed and involved in the schedules of their own bands to come along and 'guest' - being 'honoured' to do so - on a Dusty Springfield session. To do so in those days would also have been unheard of.

Any vocalist - and in this case a woman to boot - was always at the mercy of the session players however 'considered' these players may have been and however many trumps they'd come up with whilst working with other vocalists and for other recording managers.

It also must be said that it seems likely - for it has happened with other artists - that the Springfield verbal communication skills are not of the greatest. Many singers who are blessed with that gift of being able to communicate to an audience in their songs clearly can't order the pizza that they THINK they want over the telephone. It stands to reason that to be able to explain a taste that you, the pizza eater, are not even clear about is a tall order. The process of making a record is, similarly, very alchemical, very organic and indeed should be. The exact ingredients are un-orderable at the outset of the feast. 'T was ever thus. However, the number of stories about Dusty being 'a

difficult cow' which have surfaced in the course of her recording career and generally rumour-mongered by men are ill-
deserved. Surely the careers of none of these men were harmed
by being involved and associated with Dusty Springfield sessions?

*"I knew no tact. I mean, if it was wrong, I just used to go
flying into the studio ... Yes, that was difficult. I didn't see it
though because I was just blundering through it. It was called
tunnel vision. I wanted it that way, so they probably went off and
said: 'What a cow!' To this day Clive Westlake (songwriter)
calls me a cow because I knew what I wanted."*

Nevertheless, there must have been at one stage the now
celebrated Fender bass player who did not understand what
Dusty was trying to describe as the sound she wanted his
instrument to produce. She had heard the sound in America. He
obviously hadn't. Dusty, as her friends confirm, does burn on a
short fuse and when pressured, an inherited proclivity Pat
Rhodes thinks definitely originating from her mother, tempers
did flare. Stubbornness in the face of requests made reasonably
enough by the woman who's paying for it all was another sure
way of igniting Dusty's blue touchpaper. A drummer one day
seemed reluctant to loosen a snare to blur the precision of his
sound. As the assaulted heroine in the pulpy novel lay ravished,
cowering, fumbling with the drawstrings of her rapidly loosening bodice, threatened by the lash of the pirate, so, that day, that
drummer saw his way to loosening his snare ...

*"I'm the kind of singer that likes to put my voice on last.
Most singers will work with the rhythm track and then an
orchestration or overdubs, whatever, will go on after the singer's done a performance. In other words, surround the singer ...
I'm the opposite. I've got no courage to do that. I like it (the track
she sings to) to be as close to production as I can make it because
I bounce off what the musicians do. I'm not asking THEM to
bounce off ME. I need THEM. If they play a great lick or if there's
some emotion in the strings at a certain point, a colour I want
to hear then my voice will do things I didn't even think about. It
reacts to emotional and symphonic qualities in things. Left
alone with a piano, bass and drums, I'll freeze. To this day, I
can't sing with a piano in someone's living room. There's got to*

be a lot of sound coming through ... There are moments of sheer exhilaration (in singing) but most of my exhilaration comes in the making of the record. I'm far more interested in the putting together of a record and the mix of a record than I am in the actual vocal performance. I've always thought of myself as being part of the band. I've always thought of being part of an orchestra. The most interesting part is the building of something. Of course, the volume you hear it at in the control room, there's no way you can recreate that when you have to sing to it. One day they're going to invent a way ... everyone else can plug into the board. I want to know when the singer can! "

But, like the looming exam or the inevitable operation and the needle that puts you to sleep going in, the moment comes and Dusty has to sing. In 1990, she declared:

"I'm paralysed by studios. I feel trapped and I feel tested. I'm not as bad as I used to be but I doubt that I will ever lose that moment of sheer unadulterated terror when you close that door behind you."

Recently, she expanded her attitude and attendant emotions when describing how she perceives and experiences the record-making process:

"The putting together, the playing, the ideas that flow, the ...'yeah! That's it! Sounds great! Put in another little bit ... maybe we'll put another guitar in here, or, it needs a different fill there' ... That's joyous to me. It's probably hell for the musicians. It's great. I much more enjoy other people making music. I get thrilled to bits and then there's that moment when we go - and I'll delay it as long as I can - 'Do you think we can put another flute on?' Anything to get away from that moment when you actually go in the studio, the door closed behind you, those double doors closed behind you. And you're on your own. It takes me a while to get over that. How can I look forward to something crazily that I find so intimidating at first? I always do it and it will be the same as long as I make records. There's always that process to break down and I always warn people that it's going to happen and they don't believe me. They say, 'You'll be fine' and not much comes out for a couple of days. Stuff comes out but it's not what I mean to come out and then something ... the switch clicks and we're off and as long as they

have patience and they believe me, people I'm working with, that's fine. But there's always that process to break down."

CHAPTER FIVE

How not to become a legend

"I'm not the legendary type. You have to become a tragic figure to become a legend - like Garland and Edith Piaf. I don't have that quality. I don't particularly want it - not if you've got to slash your wrists to get it." Dusty made this time-worn observation in 1964.

Fifteen years later, Judy Garland and Piaf were dead and Dusty was on stage at the Theatre Royal Drury Lane.

"Give a butch roar or a girlish shriek. I don't mind who does what. Sort it out for yourselves ..."

The audience was roaring its lust for another legend, however reluctant their particular legend might have been in her time. Singing on the Russell Harty Show, Dusty announced the song she was about to sing:

"This is a song for all women who've been legends in their time. Sometimes the ladies involved give too much of themselves, sometimes not enough. This song (Peter Allen's QUIET, PLEASE ...) is for all those women, no matter where they are."

Dusty's beginning and her early solo career was oriented to performance whether on stage or on television.

"I found a diary from the very early days. I was actually still with THE SPRINGFIELDS and I realised that I used to go to the hairdressers at six in the morning. Then I was always trying to buy shoes. I do remember always trying to run down

45

Bond Street trying to buy shoes, to catch a plane to go some-where ... running along Oxford Street trying to find something to wear for Ready Steady Go! or something. There weren't the pressures to sort of ... you MUST have the RIGHT Armani and the RIGHT this and that and the other. It was probably C & A's, you know."

But demonstrating one's existence in front of a paying audience is the proof of every proper pop star's pudding at some point.

"... remember, the first time I got on the bus, the first record was already a hit so I was well accepted anyway. I lived at the top of Baker Street ... luckily, it wasn't too far from the bus which used to leave from the side of Madame Tussaud's at eight o'clock in the morning. They used to joke about it because I used to arrive sort of five minutes to eight and rigidly together ... and then it was sit bolt upright all the way to Bristol or ... further afield somewhere up north - Cannock. Places with no dressing rooms. We used to get changed in the manager's office in the gallery and the only light was the flashing one outside to put your make-up on and you'd actually have to come through the gallery and down through the audience to get on stage. I can't say 'Those were the days!' because they were bloody awful.

But it was good experience. It really was ... The early tours were mostly, you know, THE SEARCHERS and BRIAN POOLE and THE TREMELOES and FREDDIE AND THE DREAMERS deliver as true as possible reproduction of their recorded work. It was Dusty's very in-depth knowledge of sound equipment and instrumentation that created the tremendous frustration she often felt.

"No on-stage monitors. Nothing, nothing, that's why I used to hate it so much. Because I always knew ... You see, if I'd have been really dumb, I would have done better in terms of my stamina. I always knew there was another way. It's just that no one had invented it yet ... The tour didn't have it. Whatever tour it was didn't have it. Not here. Maybe they had it in The States, although I wonder. No, there was no sound so you were just going out bluffing, really ... Because I just couldn't stand the fact that people couldn't hear and I would spend half my time at sound checks for what they're worth running around into the

*audience but never being able to explain it and being a trouble-
maker for even mentioning it. I've got ears, you know. I've got
really good ears - terrible eyes but great ears - and I always
believed that it must be such a disappointment for people to
come, pay money - probably saved it up - and then not be able
to hear. I just think that's a rip-off. But they (the sound people)
would think they'd got it right. Never took into account that two
thousand people would deaden it. But they never bothered to
alter it once it was set at four o'clock in the afternoon. That was
it. It didn't matter who came on stage or how many people there
were in the audience, there was no adjustment. It was on or it
was off - mostly off. I don't know how we all got through it. "*

Sound checks - that moment where the 'the old one two'
comes into its own - took on a meaning of their own on Dusty's
tours. They frequently turned into rehearsals which went on
longer than the show itself and Dusty's insistence on getting 'it'
right led her into vocalising to the pitch and intensity of a
performance. The human larynx is made for only so much. The
untrained human larynx is made for even less.

Pat Rhodes confirms that a show may have been sell-out,
knock out, but Dusty only had to hear one dissenting, mildly
critical voice about the fact that the sound 'where WE were
sitting' wasn't perfect than the following day she would remike
the band and the orchestra to try and correct the tiny percentage
imperfection.

Pat is also fulsome in her elaboration of Dusty's assiduous
attention to fans and members of the audience who would come
round backstage after a show for autographs and is more than
pleased to confirm Dusty's own sentiments.

*"At Greaseborough, I finished my forty minute act, left the
stage and started to change my clothes. They started banging on
tin trays like a prison riot. I had to get dressed again and go back
on stage ... There she was (a young mum) with her scampi and
chips and I could tell she was enjoying my songs so much.
Overworked as she was, swollen ankles and all, I was her big
night out. That's why I used to go out and do it."*

That's the sort of communication where nothing needs to
be said. When words are all, Dusty acknowledges her inadequa-
cies:

"I'm shy when I'm talking. I'm suddenly out of my depth so I start making stupid noises and falling about or else I get aggressive, which suggests a big inferiority complex. But on stage, I really come alive. It's like an injection of some drug if someone says, 'I liked you'. 'I enjoyed you.' I don't see what else I do it for. It isn't the money and the rest is just slogging."

Hearing Dusty saying this, my mind leaps ahead fifteen years to SANDRA, the Californian housewife and my heart, as Dusty's, bleeds. It is little wonder that so many of her audience have stuck with Dusty for so long. They must have gone away each thinking they'd had a little piece of her other than the performance.

"I'd love to have an easy time on stage but it never works out that way. I really need the audience to lift me up and they do. It's a wonderful feeling."

"... if someone smiles when I'm singing, if someone looks at me and I'm close to them, then I want to jump up and down. I think it's because I wanted to be liked when I was a kid. I can't do anything else. On stage it's some kind of growth that happens and I know this is what I'm meant to do."

Dusty would stay behind in the theatre often into the small hours signing autographs and handing out photographs and just talking to people. Tiring work, draining every ounce of Dusty's nervous energy but essential for someone who feels they have to give one hundred and one percent of their effort. Exhausting ... and exhausting for everyone around her. But Dusty was always a nightowl.

Marcelle Bernstein, interviewing and writing about the Dusty Springfield phenomenon for the OBSERVER in the mid-sixties watched one night at the Cranbury Fold Inn, high above Blackburn in Lancashire: *'Afterwards, fans queue patiently outside her dressing room. Apart from the locals there are regular followers. A short Scot who took his holiday in Darwen to watch her every night, an eighteen year old boy whose only aim in life is earning enough money to see her shows and an aggressively plump girl with a flashlight on a cheap camera. They're shepherded in. "Could you give us a photo for my little girl?" "Will you put, TO JIM on this one?" She signs them all ... Dusty begins to wilt behind the smile and the last photograph is signed. She puts on sighted sunglasses. For the first time that evening she can see clearly and gathers up paper carriers, dresses, make-up case, an elaborate pink cake covered with roses from a fan and a bunch of flowers from a man who has sent six already. She returns to the hotel to sit up 'til four eating cold chicken while an enraptured waiter hovers round the champagne bucket.'*

It has always struck me as odd that jokes can be properly made about short-sightedness and yet not about blindness. 'She's as blind as a bat' means that the butt of the joke is short-sighted, NOT blind. Blind, she would be conveniently ignored. It is no joke being short-sighted to the extent that your movements are impaired. Dusty has always suffered with short sight. She has tried contact lenses but, Pat Rhodes told me, made Dusty's eyes water and consequently ruined the make-up. But her myopia does account for those wondrously still performances. Dusty performed where she got to, where she was put. Staircases on a set must have been a nightmare. Being unable to see your interviewer or even your fellow performers or just someone in Sainsbury's causes a certain withdrawal. Confidence is very limited by physical factors, however unseen and career opportunities become limited by the nature of the disability. Acting wouldn't have been that easy for her ... If there is little reaction on film or television to the close facial acting work involved, the communication of the required feeling is compromised. Dancing and moving other than very much on the spot is similarly seriously curtailed. And yet, we wouldn't have wanted her to wear specs, would we?

There was very little telly in those days as far as pop music was concerned but what there was, Dusty dominated although, as I have pointed out, she probably couldn't have seen just how wide her dominion stretched. It took shape and form in READY STEADY GO!

As I write, it is January 1994. Those who are presently under the age of forty will have no conception of the significance of those three little words ...

The weekend starts here! Ready ... Steady ... Go!

Rediffusion was the company which made the programme

which was broadcast on the ITV network. The content of the show wasn't merely another television version of the Variety show with pop instead of variety performers It was about fashion, style, dancing (Patrick Kerr and Theresa Confrey), hairstyles, make-up and it was about controlled freedom. It put young Great Britain in touch with itself. It was oracular. Vicki Wickham produced the show and booked the acts. Vicki and Dusty have been friends for over thirty years and Vicki has managed Dusty's career since 1987.

"I think a really stupid sense of humour (made us such good friends). We've both got a sort of very black, sick sense of humour. There was something ... the music ... I learned a helluva lot from Dusty about music. We're about ... we ARE the same age and we had some friends in common. And you must remember, this is the sixties when the music business was very small so you tended to kind of really know everybody in the business. You really did. You all went to the same places, you all knew the same people so it wasn't very hard ... With a few things in common, you became pretty firm friends quite fast. 'Course, the first single, I ONLY WANT TO BE WITH YOU, went on through every single. She became an absolute ... y'know every time she had a record out she would be on READY STEADY GO and why not? She was absolutely right for the show, off-centre which we always tried to be. We always tried to stay away from people who were a bit predictable and she certainly wasn't ... I would think it (RSG) was vital. It was a great vehicle for her and especially as she was so much part of it ... and, you know, as through everything, it's not easy for a solo ... It's not easy for women. We won't get into a whole conversation about that but it really isn't easy and I think having the vehicle of television on a fairly regular basis, especially the type of audience ... It was very cool ... the show. I mean it definitely sold records but it definitely was cool and it gave her credibility et cetera and so, yes ... I think it was, yes ... I'm sure she would say it was important in her life. To Dusty, in reality, I think there is so much talent and the records were so damned good that with or without READY STEADY GO, that with or without any television, nobody at Radio could have refused to play it and so I think she would have had equal success but I think that the television just,

obviously visually, just added to it and she became a household name and is till a household name."

The show started life in a television studio in London's Kingsway, the north eastern perimeter of the West End. There ought to be a blue plaque. People DO forget. I'm amazed Dusty has such recall.

"This is hard for me because, you know, you just went on and ... everybody. Michael Aldridge, Cathy (MacGowan). The Stones, The Beatles. You name them. They were all on it. Vicki would remember because she booked it. I was a CERTAIN influence on the booking of READY STEADY GO! unbeknownst to me because I was so enthusiastic about black acts coming over that they used to book them because I'd be raving about them so much. I'd forgotten, actually, that I'd a lot of influence over what went on, without meaning to. I was just so incredibly enthusiastic ... There were crowds outside, right? The police were always there and we'd have to have the police push the crowds back to get in and it was always ... maybe it wasn't insane for anyone else but then I was always late and so it was always; 'Is she here or isn't she?' But I actually was there. Sandie Shaw wasn't once, I remember. I had to sing the beginning of - maybe she just didn't show up or she wasn't in place on time - 'Always Something There To Remind Me'. Anyway ... So, fill, fill fill! I don't know whether that was when I was doing the compering or when it was when I was appearing. But I always managed to be there on time eventually and it was just, er ...well, one more time I must try to get it right but on READY STEADY GO! that was pretty difficult but that's what gave it its atmosphere. It was the immediacy. It was the first show that was done almost like a documentary. It was quite extraordinary and with warts and all - That's what worked. It was that sense of News about it and so the camera angles were strange and they were always the most unflattering. Rollo, was it? Lurching around? Yeah. Rollo Gamble! New Years Eve was the best because everyone was so incredibly busy. It was amazing the show got on at all. Again, you know, you'd stand on these little daises and they were so close they (the audience) used to goose you and I was really incredibly shy and to have to perform with people in your face was so totally unnatural.

Besides, they all wanted to be on camera more. You know the audience was what it was all about, to hell with the act. It was, you know, 'How's my dress and how's my hair?' They were more worried about that than probably I was. But that whole thing was innovative. I think they were actually ... were they (Rediffusion) not a News company? Essentially, and that's probably all they were capable of doing and when they went live ... my God! It was very difficult. When we had THE ANIMALS, I mean it was incredible for its time still, when you look at it. It has more immediacy than any of the gloss ones."

The other reputation Dusty garnered in those first solo years other than the one for being 'a cow' was:

"... one for being a bit of a bad girl. For throwing things (food) around but that was a hoot. I actually acted out the things that were in the slapstick films that no one had the nerve to do."

"... I did so much partying during the sixties and early seventies ..."

"If a head waiter was obsequious to me while really abusing some common waiter who was trying to do his best then I felt this great need to make a stink and hurl something at the head waiter. It was usually just a vol au vent but it inevitably missed and hit someone else which set everybody off. By the time the headline reached Australia, it would be this vast cake I had thrown when actually it was quite a delicate hors d'oeuvre (does she mean petit four?) *I thought it was funny though not everybody else did. What I liked was the chaos it caused, the way things came out of other people who were really quite prim. It was as though they'd been longing to do these things all their lives. Vicars' wives would take off their heels and start hammering their husbands over the head ..."*

Having inherited her appreciation of 'the crack' from her mother, Dusty turned into a great party-giver of her own. Cilla Black remembered going to them:

"Great family parties ... Mum and dad were always there in the midst of all the weird rock an' rollers and Bobby and me ... Lots of people used to think that girl singers were rivals but we never were. If you look back and compare the records we were totally different. There was room for all girls together to have hit records. I look back on Dusty then being a lot of fun.

Wicked sense of humour, she loved throwing cream cakes at everybody. Never threw one at me, though. She had a wicked sense of humour and still has today. She's got this incredible voice ... soul ..."

Dusty has very fond memories of the parties she gave in her Baker Street flat but I wonder just WHY she never threw a pie at 'our Cilla'?.

" They were the all-time food-fight parties. My brother always started it. THE SEEKERS' manager would always be there and she'd be wearing a low, black dress - and I knew my brother wouldn't be able to resist it. Something would just go hurtling across the room. A slice of something, cold meat or something and it would hit her and that was just at the point of the V in the back. That was the point for me to start and it was surprising the number of people who liked it who you thought would never like it and the people you thought WOULD like it left. I always believe if you give people enough food and enough drink and mix them all up, it will all work and if they don't like it they can go home. I remember Martha and The Vandellas cowering behind the couch because there was just everything flying in the air and then once they got used to it they sort of came out swinging with these huge long French loaves. God! Poached eggs - tennis racquets and poached eggs were good! How many people were in that room at any one time? Seventy five? Yes! Poor Kim Weston, she caught a load of sauerkraut (does she mean coleslaw?) or something. She came in and she just made this great entrance - like 'Hi, honey!' and went sliding across, practically out into Baker Street, off the top floor. Gene Pitney got hit with a bag of flour. He wasn't too keen. He had his best suit on. But there were people in the bath, people's clothes were shoved down the loo. I mean it was real students' stuff but it was 1963/64. It was wonderful. I do remember lobbing - or was it my brother - anyway, one or other of the O'Briens lobbed a sardine right across the room to one of the Shangri Las and she had a very deep - how do you say it - decolletage and it went straight down. I think ... No, that was the cue for the second party. Something like that had to be achieved before all hell could let loose. They were great parties. We cleaned them up didn't we, the next day? There got less and less time to be that crazy. I did

believe in therapeutic use of throwing reject china down theatre corridors. But again, I always cleaned it up, I never expected anyone to clean it up. But if you actually stand at the top of an old theatre staircase and you get, like, a gross of cups and saucers and teaspoons and - you know the stairwell where all the stairs go down like that - if you actually tip it from about eight floors up and you record it and then you put it in slow motion, it's one of the best sounds I've ever heard. Unfortunately I nearly caught the entire chorus line one time, doing that. Again, it was my brother that did it!"

For an 'incredibly shy' person, this was one way of not being a wallflower at a party, especially your own. It was without doubt, a time which can be regarded in hindsight as rosier than it was. Sardine-lobbing made for 'wild' people as far as the non-intrusive newspapers and their leashed inkhounds were concerned.

"We were such innocents, you know ... with the swinging sixties. It was chocolate swiss roll and cocoa. It was! It was, you know, none of the naughty sex-drugs-and-rock 'n' roll stuff. It was swiss roll and cocoa and a gramophone!"

Very grateful a 'sub' would have been on the news or picture desk to get a story about Britain's number one lady singer apprehended 'sardine lobbing'. Dusty was young - twenty five was still young - and forgivable. The quaint sense of 'fun' extended to practical jokes like ordering fourteen Chinese meals for fourteen unsuspecting people or sending a baby sitter round to people who didn't have any children.

But it would be all right when she settled down, wouldn't it? When she found the right man? Despite the swinging appendage, the sixties were approached by contemporary commentators (okay, call them journalists) from a standpoint on the highest moral ground. If a girl wasn't married, it wasn't assumed that she was a sexual being at all. She might be 'going out' with someone but until the ring was slipped on, nothing else was assumed to have been slipped in. The British media of the time loved Dusty Springfield. It would be all right, they must have thought. Just look at Cilla, look at Sandie, look at Lulu ...

Dusty did, every day for they were the names she gave her bigger wigs, the blonde coiffures that crowned the glory that w

CHAPTER SIX

The Call of the Wild

1965 brought three singles, all hits. YOUR HURTIN' KIND OF LOVE in February, MIDDLE OF NOWHERE in June and SOME OF YOUR LOVIN' in September. It seems the girl could do no wrong.

In 1964, Dusty had collapsed from exhaustion. Afterwards, she pronounced:

"I'm all right physically but I'm still trying to adjust myself to life. My trouble is that I live totally on my nerves. My mother always said I didn't have much stamina and I've found out that she was right."

Pat Rhodes is at great pains for it to be understood how much Dusty functions on a huge outpouring of energy. This stream of energy is entirely self-generated but it doesn't come from nowhere. It has to be supported. The slightest jolt or threat to the sources of that energy and the system will collapse.

"The minute Dusty is left alone," Pat says, *"she's like a lost child. She needs company and affection. She has an extremely small circle of friends - you could count them on one hand."*

Dusty's business affairs and the day-to-day management of her career was overseen by Vic Billings. Pat Rhodes thinks that it was Dusty who found Vic rather than the other way around and, initially, they signed a management agreement lasting, Pat believes, for a year and then signed for a further five.

Dusty's performance bookings and contracts were handled still by agents. This is quite usual. Management often merely oversees the bookings of artists in live performance, having no hand in the direct dealings with the promoter of the concert or the club owner/booker at the cabaret venue. Dusty had already poached Pat Rhodes from Emlyn Griffiths to work exclusively for her. She had always noticed how efficiently Pat ran the busy office. Pat remembers that Dusty always said to her that when she was on her own, she would have Pat work for her and her alone. Pat always thought she was joking but Dusty was as good as her word.

Organising the Springfield schedule cannot have been easy. Dusty is not someone who has ever complied with the hours other people keep. She has ideas and remembers things often in the middle of the night, telephoning her thoughts unaware that it is three in the morning and the person at the other end of the 'phone is fast asleep. All right if you are un-married or unattached and have no other ties. Pat was unmarried in the early days and was able to devote the necessary time and attention to Dusty's whimsical, organic methods of working. Tolerance of such vagaries is an essential qualification for anyone working in any capacity in artists' management. The apparent eccentricities and enabling these to fit into the schedules of business life are the very grist to the management mill.

Pat worked with Dusty from whichever flat or house the self-confessed itinerant Miss Springfield was living in at the time. Vic, on the other hand, worked out of a very small office in Paddington. Dusty's solo debut had been into a music industry where management and management profile had not become the byword it became in the later sixties and seventies when the managers were often just as celebrated as their artists. It was at least a continuous, if not a particularly forceful, business situation. Vic, sadly no longer with us, understood Dusty and was able to accommodate her capricious way of working.

"I run on emotions and emotions being what they are, they're not constant. At least, mine aren't therefore I must be hell to work with ..."

By 1964, Dusty had established herself as a very big star

indeed. Compared to today, the treadmill of work and the hectic schedule with which she complied is unthinkable. THE BEATLES had spearheaded the vanguard of the British invasion of the American music business and successful British artists now automatically encompassed the Atlantic horizon. But it was a long time ago; 1964 BV. Before Video. You had to go and DO it.

"I want to go on notching up hits in the American charts. It's a personal ambition, really. No special reason but when you see yourself in the charts over there you can tell yourself you're doing all right."

Doing it meant television music shows, chat and talk shows which format didn't even figure on British TV at the time. There were also live shows.

"I did a lot of stuff in The States. I did all of those shows that were the equivalents of READY STEADY GO! SHINDIG, SHIVAREE, SHEBANG and they always seemed to be in somewhere god-awful on location, like the Riverside Racetrack in a temperature of 118 centigrade and they'd put those lights up, you know, those huge silver (mirrored) balls and you were supposed to look glamourous. It was, usually ... You know that scene in the film NASHVILLE where they're singing in the middle of the racetrack. That's exactly what it was like. They never did it in the same place like READY STEADY GO! ... It was pure Robert Altman, it really was."

America was also the land of radio and, in those days the radio stations which were responsible for making the hits before MTV was even thought of had themselves realised the extra promotional mileage that could be obtained from their being associated with presenting the performers of the hits they were creating live in front of a paying public. Murray Kaufman was a famous New York radio disc jockey.

"It was the era of Beatlemania and Murray (the K) Kaufman liked to consider himself the fifth Beatle. He thought I was from Liverpool and decided that he'd got to have me."

The venue that Dusty was booked into for this Murray Kaufman Promotion was the Fox Theatre Brooklyn. The Fox was a working cinema but the extra live shows were very, very popular.

"I think they were still using the cinema sound. Probably with a few speakers on stage but it was cavernous, that stage because behind the (movie) screen was this huge area and the band would be behind it. I don't remember the sound there being any better than the sound at the Cannock Odeon although it probably was because Murray (the K) was involved. But I do remember that the time lag there was so awful so it could not have been that good. You know, the drummer appeared to you to be half a beat behind because he was so far back in the bowels of the Brooklyn Fox. There'd be six shows a day but only two songs, you see. They'd show a film and then they'd show the stage show and then a film and then the stage show. That's how they did it. It went on until about one in the morning, right? That's how they did that stuff. But they'd start so early. Oh, God! What a nightmare! I had laryngitis and I had to sing WISHIN' AND HOPIN' at ten o'clock in the morning. That's a nightmare, for the audience as well!"

Many artists would have been daunted by the invitation, Dusty leapt at Murray (the K)'s like a ravening tigress onto her first oxo cube.

"It was a dream come true. It was priceless. I would've paid to do it. I was the token whitey. The token honky. They were very affectionate - if someone caused me any trouble, they'd say: 'Don't lean on her. She's with US.' I blundered my way through Harlem not knowing what was around me, a beehive surrounded by pimps, hookers and addicts and pushers. I stayed at the Hotel Teresa with broken windows and Malcolm X was staying there. God protects fools and innocents."

Oh, I wish ...

"There were a couple of other white acts on the show. I think Jay and The Americans were there ... Murray hedged his bets with a few white acts. I mostly hung out with THE RONETTES ... and shared a dressing with them which was an extraordinary experience! Y'know, it was like a hundred and four degrees in this very, very small dressing room and all our beehives were in there - three black beehives and one white one. It was collisions constantly. Next door were MARTHA and THE VANDELLAS and, the other side, were THE SUPREMES. I remember Mary Wilson was always reading Latin books and Diana Ross's mum helped

me turn my hems up because I was always buying things that were too long."

And, don't forget that British wannabee ... She was still wanting to be ...

"... to stand in the wings and be able to ... there's always an odd Vandella missing because they used to do off-stage back-ups for Marvin Gaye and there was always a part of (sings) 'Hitchike, hitchike, baby' missing. One Vandella would have a hangover or something so I got to be a Vandella but I never got to be onstage as a Vandella."

"I had a lot of good times, very heady times being involved in that period. After all, what could be more stimulating than listening to the brass arrangements of the TEMPTATIONS from the side of the stage. That was heaven for me. Mind you, I didn't like performing there or anything else but I wanted to stand at the side of the stage and soak it all up so that I could use it. I knew all the routines and knew exactly how to sound like a Vandella ... and a SHIRELLE if it came to that. I know how to do that stuff to this day. I can still go off into my Shirley Alston (SHIRELLE) impression. Whoever it was I wanted to be. I'd slavishly copy them because we hadn't caught on to them in this country so I could get away with it."

"It was pretty overwhelming but I just sort of went along with it. I was always protected from any trouble there might have been around me. I hadn't got a clue what was going on. We used to land up in all night bars and party and it was great. I never got in any trouble whatsoever. Just was nice people. Now, whether in retrospect they were just humouring me or not ... But I didn't care. I was just having a really good time soaking up the influences. Claudine ... Claudette? Smokey's wife. Claudette ... They were always cooking up on the top floor and would always invite me up. It was a marvellous time."

Dusty was obviously unafraid and her shyness seems to have left her. I know several people of Dusty's nature who, in some strange way, were liberated by socialising with another race but from the joyousness which comes through all these quotes, it seems more that Dusty felt that she had in that same strange way, 'come home'.

Human beings can often feel that they have been born into

the wrong skin, even at the wrong time. They can certainly feel that they've been born into the wrong culture in the wrong countries. Arriving in New York, finding herself predominantly with women and NOT having to compete as the ONLY girl all the time must have been tremendously liberating. It must have shown Dusty what COULD have been.

In Britain she had enjoyed being dubbed - I believe it was by Cliff Richard - 'the White Negress', a sobriquet which personally I find shudderingly patronising but which was fallen upon by the British music press who thought the appellation the bee's knees. I have to admit I've never understood it. Ray Coleman has quoted the example of Mary Wells refusing to believe until she saw the album cover that Dusty Springfield was white. Certain inflections, an overall 'brown' character maybe, certain of the vocal gymnastics redolent of a black, (and much later) gospel-invoked STYLE perhaps, but a BLACK voice? I believe that it was the old fallback of only being able to describe something in terms of something else. What's wrong with unique? Dusty appears to have felt indifferently.

"I certainly wasn't offended ... In fact I don't think it had any impact on me at all. However, it's not much fun having a glass of whisky thrown in your face by Nina Simone who called me a honky and resented me being alive! She was having a few problems which I thought I could solve by being nice. Huh. I was still as naive as ever. I was on a crusade of being helpful to people who had problems and I was warned not to approach her but ... I knew better, didn't I?"

But the girls with whom she shared backstage life at The Fox and whom she so admired must, in their turn, have thought Dusty pretty special too. So, Nina Simone didn't like her? So what? Nina Simone don't like nobody much. Never has. In general, Nina apart, Dusty must have been thrilled with this proper 'blackening' her reputation received, probably to the point of the whole experience being life-changing. It was certainly a great vindication of her work and just cause for celebration.

"I brought my parents over, the first time my mother had ever been on a 'plane. We just filled her full of brandy and she was fine! It was really odd, you know, out there in Flatbush with

my parents. Just bizarre, you know, with Martha and The Vandellas and ... er ... I can't remember because the show changed about every six days. I mean, other people would come in. I don't think Stevie Wonder was in that one. I used to go to The Apollo too and watch Joe Tex and Sugar Pie De Santa and hang out round the back. I was just in awe. I loved Martha's voice. It had a richness that some of the other groups didn't have. But some of the people that I DIDN'T work with like the VELVELETTES and the MARVELETTES, they affected me. Those early girl, black girl-group records, PLEASE MR. POSTMAN and all that. Most of all the SHIRELLES. I wanted to be Shirley too, you see. I was going through these schizophrenic vocal changes between wanting to be BABY WASHINGTON and Shirley. (Sings) 'Mama said there'd be days like this, there's be days like this my mama said, mama said, mama said ...' I thought it was all so precise but actually when you look back to a lot of that, it wasn't as precise as you thought it was ... They were on ... What was that woman - Florence Greenberg. They were on a yellow label, Sceptre. Now, you see, that was the other thing ... Didn't Dionne start there? Yeah, yeah, Chuck Jackson, now we're talking. Tommy Hunt, yeah. That's where I first heard I JUST DON'T KNOW WHAT TO DO WITH MYSELF. There was a whole early Motown. Sceptre was before, just before. Yeah ... Chicago, New York. There were various schools of music developing and, you know, a little later the Philadelphia thing was happening. But Sceptre, I suppose, actually, would be my strongest influences a little earlier than that because there was THE SHIRELLES and DION."

The Dusty we hear talking through these lines fairly bubbles with enthusiasm. She sounds like a fan and, indeed, she has based her career on being a fan. She is incredibly generous when she likes something or someone. Pat Rhodes sees it as the need to give out as much love as possible in order to get the most back. Dusty needs to love and to be loved and taking time out for other people, listening to them, being appreciative is the best way to be loved back. The loving of the self, a quality also not unknown in Miss Springfield, is often commutable into second place when Dusty falls in love - with a song, a band, a sound, a place, a person. A record label.

"I think I was aware of it before it became Motown. There were several labels before one was Gordy. Well, there was Tamla and there was another one ... I think it was probably with acts like THE CONTOURS, (sings) 'Do you love me?' when that first happened and SHOUT. They weren't on Gordy when they did SHOUT. Those early... I mean they were REALLY rough, those records but they had an energy and a sound unlike anything I've heard before."

These early American experiences certainly cemented her love affair with Motown and, upon returning to England, she started her campaign to achieve for the label and its artists the recognition she thought they deserved and weren't yet receiving in Great Britain.

"It was so obviously better than a lot of things that were happening. They were really good songs done extremely rhythmically. It was the first time there had been that kind of song structure. Some of them were sloppy but it was this sloppiness which made them attractive. I noticed a lot of it was to do with the bass player, the drummer's licks, Holland Dozier Holland and musicians like Jim Jamerson if you were lucky. That was the motor of motorcity. You could put anything on top of it and it would still sound like Motown. The artists were probably secondary and certainly there were a lot of people who sang but who didn't last. Whether it was because they got worn out by the situation, I don't know. They were talented and certainly you could put all sorts of people over a splendid bass line and have a hit."

" ... it was just, this factory, as you know. I mean, the stories one gets to hear about people being brought back at gunpoint to sing off a tour and the tracks were always recorded in keys far too high - especially for THE FOUR TOPS - which gave it that incredible energy because he was always grasping for these keys that were too high for him because nobody had bothered to ask him ... They were just made like a conveyor belt. I mean, I met one percussion player who'd been playing for Motown for about fifteen years and had never met Diana Ross, never met anyone, never met a singer. They would churn this stuff out and then go, 'Now, who'd sound good on that?' or 'Who do we have this week?', 'Who can we get off the Harold Theatre

in Washington between four and six o'clock?'. And they'd fly them back or whatever - drive them back! - and record them and put them back on the stage the next day or whatever and how they managed it, I don't know. I mean, hit after hit after hit after hit ..."

Generally, it is to be acknowledged that Motown would never have been as successful as it became without white audiences to augment the homeboys and girls who were its heartbeat.

"It was only later that Motown became glossy and I liked it more and more because it was ... nobody made a sound like that, nobody played the bass like that, nobody recorded the drums as if they were recorded in a large trash can. Nobody did those fills. They were supremely good and nobody wrote strings like that and nobody wrote horns like that. Nobody had been that seamless in pop music before and they were good tunes too. I mean, the hooks of THE SUPREMES records, everyone could sing them and that's when it started crossing over genuinely. Basically, Motown became black music for white people. That's where it got its biggest success."

Dusty is characteristically modest about what she has to know was her enormous contribution.

"I'm sure I did a bit of PR for the artists but I wasn't responsible for getting it on television. It had a lot to do with Vicki Wickham, I think and the READY STEADY GO! situation. It was a natural progression to do a special. The acts had been coming over and doing things so it made a lot of sense. It was amazing to get something like that together ..."

"I'm given to enormous fits of enthusiasm and it doesn't matter, you know ... I'm not in the business of PR but I would just talk about them endlessly and they were running MY motor, so to speak. So, it never occurred to me that I was doing PR for them. I was just entranced. So if I had something to do with it, it's only in hindsight and having been told by them from time to time that they really liked what I said about them. But it really is only in hindsight."

As well as duetting with Martha Reeves, Dusty ended up hosting THE SOUND OF MOTOWN, the television spin-off of the Motown Revue in March 1965.

"It (the revue) was too advanced. Motown audiences in the States get an enormous proportion of coloured people and, of course, there isn't such a large one here. And the majority of the acts weren't sufficiently well-known here. They knew THE SUPREMES of course and had just about heard of MARTHA but the rest of the acts were unknown to the average customer."

Motown magic may not have been immediately successful in Britain but it didn't take long. Motown were grateful; they sent Dusty a jewelled collar for her dog. But she never climbed on board. Kiki Dee did. Kiki was also managed by Vic Billings.

"The climate wasn't right. I would have been intimidated because I was in awe of them and I don't sing well when I'm in awe. I usually sing better in England ... (Ha Ha). In retrospect I'm glad they didn't (ask me) because I might have accepted and I wanted to stumble along on my own. Make my own blunders."

I wish I'd had friends like Dusty although I wouldn't have bothered spending the precious thought time in company conference to dream up the jewelled dog collar gift. I'd have just given her a percentage.

"The ones that affected me most, actually, were not even the vocal ones but the later, the Junior Walker records and things like that. That came the closest to all night dancing for me ... we were dancing all night in Sydney to Junior Walker. Road Runner ... Still the greatest record ..."

CHAPTER SEVEN

Arriva! Arriva!

The fruits of success can be enjoyed anywhere and there's nothing like a holiday to reward hard work. Dusty has always loved to travel. She has ascribed it to the heritage she claims from the Irish tinkers who were her ancestors, wandering Ireland in the Celtic mists, presumably in horse drawn vans. I would imagine Dusty prefers the twentieth century version made by Boeing.

One of them took her to Rio. The trip remains one of her sharper memories. Having been brought up with Tom's love of Brazilian music, getting to go there must have been a thrill indeed.

"My brother went ... Who else went? Martha? Did she come? Yeah, but I can't remember who else. I remember Martha being there because we had a picture taken of Coco Vada, you know the big, big statue of Christ that overlooks Rio and she's standing there and she's got gold lame pants on. I do remember that and a headscarf and I think I had a head scarf because it was windy up there and you know, the beehive ... I didn't want to see it floating - flying down to Rio! It was very bizarre. There was somebody else there ... It's all a bit of a blur. It was the greatest, That was before it got truly violent. I mean, now, it's actually quite dangerous and it's also got extremely touristy - Remember this was 1964, maybe, before it became such a massively commercialised thing. Anyway, I've never had feelings like that before or since. Just being incredibly high on music ... they

rehearse all year round, for each district, small district has its own band and they go onto this parade ground. At the end is like a collecting ring for all the bands and they're all rehearsing in there, they're getting ready for the parade before ... and they all, one at a time, come out of the collecting area and go through these vast bleachers of people and they're all dancing and playing and there may be forty drummers and they never get in each others' way. Just forty drummers and then the trombones and the dancers - It's just brilliant and I went and crawled into the collecting ring, through the police and everything because, you know, they just hit people, the police down there. They're always picking up broken bodies. White-helmeted police, they don't care, you know, they just hit you. But I managed to get away from them and went into the collecting ring. I've never experienced a feeling like it. I mean, it was just insanity but it was sheer joy of the sound and the rhythms. Nothing, nothing has ever been like it again. And it was great until I was dancing in bare feet and I trod on a broken bottle and that was the end of my trip to Rio. But actually, I stayed up for three days and three nights dancing and didn't drink a thing. It was purely just the drug of the music and to this day there is nothing that will make me get crazier or dance more than hearing a Samba band. It's fantastic. There are so many different kinds of music. Even within Brazil, there are different regional musics ... There is a style that is pure street Samba and it's not, you know, polite. It's savage and tribal and it really is. It's unlike anything else. Nothing else is like it in the world."

You can hear the country and its vibrant, colourful culture bubbling through Dusty's own enraptured words. But there were other countries, not quite as fondly remembered.

Entanglements with police in faraway places occurred more than once in those mid-sixties. Dusty's press was handled by Keith Goodwin, a former journalist who had set up his own Publicity Management Office in Monmouth Street. In late 1964, his telephone must have been ringing off the hook. Dusty had arrived in South Africa.

"I could jump off Tower bridge if I wanted my name in the papers. I would hardly put the whole ECHOES show out of work for publicity. I've been to America four times already. I don't

need this type of publicity. I did not break any laws, it was agreed that I should appear before multi-racial audiences."

I think the fuss really upset her. Defiant and rebellious Dusty, always ready to spring to the defence of the put-upon waiter, ready to bristle at the scantest social sleight had decided to tour in South Africa. In South Africa, even now, being served, being waited on is, for many, like a drug. It is required to confirm status, to establish social supremacy ... I have seen it recently in full finger-snapping fettle and it's a disease!

"I always did blunder into things. I wasn't making any major statement, I just felt better about it that way being the naive person I was. I thought it (determining her contract with a South African promoter) was morally the right thing to do. But they were waiting for 'some idiot' to write a very small clause into their contract; they were so goddam smart. There was a real backlash because I was accused of making things worse and so, unwittingly, I had. But what meant something to me was the airline workers, the black guys, lifted their hats when I got onto the 'plane. I thought; 'Oh. You DID notice even though I fucked it up ..."

Recently she has expounded the events as she remembers them more fully:

"... All through the sixties I was incredibly naive about all sorts of things, politics being one of them. Subsequently my biggest interest is geo-politics but THEN I was floundering through things and I had 'ideals'. So, in my contract, I put in, in small print, that I wouldn't play to segregated audiences and it all went very quiet and I thought' 'Wow! I've achieved it'. When the band and I got off the plane, the South African government people were standing under the wings of the plane thrusting these bits of paper at us to sign to say that we would do exactly as they said we would do and that was that we had no right to come into the country and make trouble - blah, blah, blah - and that the contract as it stood was null and void. So naturally, none of us signed. ... The promoter had found a loophole that I didn't know about. It's highly technical in that mixed audiences could be allowed in cinemas if it was a live show for some reason. So, the promoter who was a good guy had sorted these venues out ... With which - I'm quite, I don't know, I can't prove it - I

imagine the South African government went, 'Whoops! We've missed this one.' It was a severe embarrassment to them at the time and basically there's no way that blacks were going to come to my shows anyway - they didn't know who I was. (And nor would they have been able to afford the ticket prices!) The odd mixed race person would have come but what happened was, when we opened in Johannesburg there were security people going round the audience counting the number of (Cape) coloureds as they were called - and still are. Mixed race. I think there were probably about five or six, maybe ten. I don't know, I wasn't counting. They didn't say much. But when we got to Cape Town, they just put us under what I would call hotel arrest. The shows were off and as they politely put it, something like ...'withdraw the right for you to stay here for more than twenty four hours' or something like that. The promoter was desperately trying to sort this out and it went to about three or four days ... I never want to see another tomato sandwich - that's what they kept sending up to the room. Tomato sandwiches ... and in the end that sort of drummed us out of the country but they didn't deport us because if they deport you they have to pay your fares. After that two things happened. The promoter gave up and moved his family to Israel and what happened was that that loophole got closed so I didn't do it an ounce of good. But I didn't really go there to do good. I went there to sing and I had, somewhere, this really naive ideal that perhaps being there would make some kind of a difference. Well, it didn't. For a while it made it worse and I think those were the accusations I got for making trouble and my records were taken off South African radio for years and out of the shops for many years."

Certain British actors and impresarios, notably Derek Nimmo who frequently toured and therefore earned a large part of their living from overseas work in such English-speaking countries as South Africa, condemned her action, one of the first seen as the kind of protest that would gradually isolate South Africa culturally and through this ostracism ultimately force the ruling white elite to change their laws. How long it will take for them to change their finger-snapping, Hey-Boy attitudes is an entirely different matter.

Are you listening, Nina Simone? Honkeys may have been

to blame in the first place but lotsa honkeys did something to change it.

However, any change in the law would take another thirty years to accomplish but, above all, let's remember that Dusty was in there slugging at the beginning. About Nimmo in 1990, Dusty was unequivocally still angry:

"What a prat! Is he still alive? Well, he's still a prat. I would say it to his face!"

She must have been very disappointed at the brickbats that were hurled. People didn't rally round.

"No. No. Equity were okay. It was the musicians union that were with me on that one. Originally they thought it was a great idea but when I came back, I just got slanged left right and centre by Max Bygraves and people like that who were, I suppose, worried about my closing down some form of work for them. I just wasn't thinking about any of that stuff. There may have been some people who rallied round. But there's a part of me that, although I fear for the future of South Africa, I would just like to be there for the day of the elections. Even if I just flew in for the day and sat in a hotel, because it's a long time."

The huge press attention that the episode primed was almost the first indication in the media that certain journalists in the chattering and opinion-forming classes were beginning to think that behind Dusty Springfield lay a more serious phenomenon than they had hitherto assessed. The rose had thorns.

"Whatever your personal political feelings are, if you become involved in them publicly, you're bound to come out the loser," Dusty said in 1964.

Girls and politics and black people ... Tut, tut, tut. Read between Tito Burns' lines as he felt he had to defend his client.

"She has very strong feelings about this colour business. Dusty's a pretty deep-thinking girl. I'm fully behind her in everything she does in this matter."

Sweet of him to stand behind her. But girls were beginning to be 'pretty deep-thinking' ... they'd been doing so, somewhat un-noticed by men, for a good few tens of thousands of years. But thanks for the support, Tito and all you other good ol' boys.

It would be interesting, one day, to know the whole story about the South Africa trip. London showbusiness has tight and direct family links to that of South Africa. Tito Burns was never anyone's fool yet knowing Dusty's insistence on 'that clause', was this (in hindsight, of course) a test to see what would happen? South Africa would have been a lucrative market for Western music acts but 'some idiot' had to be chosen and an idiot who would stick to their guns and not cave in under pressure ...

On a purely artistic level, given the 'Zulu tunes' that were available, given Dusty's ethnic musical curiosity, it is such a crying shame that she and the rest of the world have been starved for so long of the music and rhythms that emanate from that beautiful but burdened land, music which Dusty must have been aware of in the sixties as pioneered by people such as Miriam Makeba and beginning to be exported by such as Jeremy Taylor.

CHAPTER EIGHT

Without a song ...

1966 was a year that saw four singles but no new album although Phillips issued a GOLDEN HITS compilation in October. The singles were LITTLE BY LITTLE, YOU DON'T HAVE TO SAY YOU LOVE ME, GOIN' BACK and ALL I SEE IS YOU. As another very good song says, 'It was a very good year ...'

"I just go for the jugular with songs. I mean, songs with me are right if they sound right, if they affect my emotions, if they affect me emotionally. If they make me happy or if they make me sad. I still live on my emotions. I'm not very clinical about ... or very calculated. I mean, if something's doing that to me AND it's commercial then I'm the happiest woman in the world."

I cannot even conceive of the number of times Dusty must have heard the line about, 'Have I got a song for YOU!' Though spanning only eight years, Dusty's career had already seen the demise of Tin Pan Alley and the emergence of songwriting as a recognisable and respectable cultural development in terms of the West. It had been indubitably spearheaded and made credible by THE BEATLES. Wiggy intellectuals were beginning to argue the relative merits and demerits of whether or not THE BEATLES' songs were art. When that starts to happen, you KNOW it's making money for someone that someone else isn't getting!

"When I discovered other music, it was people who were fairly obscure in this country who influenced me. Singers like Baby Washington and Mitti Collier who had, what I call, big brown voices. Baby Washington ... you would never have known her records at all then. They weren't famous here (Britain) at all. CHAINED TO A MEMORY. ONLY THOSE IN LOVE. THAT'S HOW HEARTACHES ... I used to cover all these things and put them on albums. They were all early records, like Garnet Mimms and THE ENCHANTERS. They were great records. Those were our biggest influences. Things which didn't mean a thing in this country. But I knew that's what I wanted to do so I did and they were like pale copies of them but that was novel in this country. 'Where did you find that song, Dusty?' 'I swiped it off Garnet Mimms!'".

But Dusty's metamorphosis from lead to solo singer had been made with the help of the tried and tested. Both Ivor Raymonde and Clive Westlake (Pit a Pat) had written for THE SPRINGFIELDS.

"There were various songwriters who definitely were writing in a style that made sense for me. Ivor (Raymonde) was one at the beginning and then Clive came in with the 'I'm going to write an Italian ballad even if I'm Welsh' routine. And you know, he was very clever ..."

Other than from her own backyard, publishers must have been queuing to send her songs.

"Essentially, what we were all doing was copying the influences and adapting them. In actual fact, making a damn good stab at trying to sound that way but not being quite able to do it which is how this whole sound came about. The British sound and then it got exported back to The States with a slant on it and it became massively successful ..."

When all's said and done, I have to accept that the commercial pop song is bound to be take its shape and form and hue inside a trellis of basic cliche. The viable lyrical images are defined by the medium which itself is defined by the need to perpetuate the idea of romantic love itself, keep it rosy red, flowery fresh, alive and tangible and ongoing for it is on its very narrow shoulders that the whole of our society in the West is based. People of opposite sex are attracted to each other, fall chastely in love, marry as virgins, engender children, live monogamously, happily together until death does them part whence one will follow the other because love cannot exist unless the lovers be reunited in heaven. Upon that proposition rests our laws and, in turn, upon that foundation stands an awful lot of property and the ownership of a huge amount of wealth.

So, to keep that little lot afloat, you can't really THINK too much about pop songs and thus the songs that mirror the idyll have to have some pretty hefty hooks on which to hang the populace! They also have to have the ability to allow the listeners, having taken the romantic plunge, to recognise their regrets without then rocking the boat too much. If you can make 'em cry, they're less likely to get angry.

"A good love song has to make me cry. There's a connection between the pit of my stomach and my eyes. That's the Irish melancholy in me. A song has to be immediate. It cannot grow on me - once it sends a message to my tear ducts, then it's right."

It now seems weirdly wonderful that the majority of the pop songs up until the middle sixties were songs written by men. In Dusty's case, I find it doubly ironic that men wrote songs for women to sing and that the songs were about how men think that women feel (should feel) about men. There were so few women writing songs themselves. Most who did, wrote with men. It interests me that the reflective, nay introspective, GOIN' BACK released in July 1966 was sandwiched between a couple of belting pop marching hymns.

I have found very little reference in the material I have had to hand about Dusty's theatricality. I don't mean her waving her arms about a lot and stamping around and losing her rag. I'm talking about the actor in her. I'm talking about the thought processes which quite naturally, instinctively, kick-in to play when she approaches a song.

We've looked at the way she works, at the way she puts together her recordings, constructing them from, often, improvised inspirations, working off the abilities that the musicians create on the day. It's no different from the way Peter Hall or Trevor Nunn directs a play except they use actors and not musicians. They employ an actor because they know that actor will do what is basically wanted and then some ...

"... I always do records in bits and pieces, because my ultimate aim is to string as many good bits together as possible. Which is what I try to do. It's not that the next bit after a really good bit is bad, it's the bit before that was SO good that I can't follow it and that sounds very conceited. I can't live up to it and so I like to do things a bit at a time. I'm no good at going all the way through."

In the theatre, that process is known as 'Rehearsals'.

In her particular theatrical context, Dusty works up to her own form of 'first night', exploring her text, seeing where the parameters lie, knowing what it is she needs to bring out of the work to be able to communicate that essence most effectively to her audience. She doesn't just sing, she performs. She has an actor's insecurity, not a singer's nerves. She has a director's breadth of sensitivity and awareness of the totality of her work; she doesn't merely stand at the mike and belt. She knows EVERYTHING that CAN go wrong, she's not merely worried about her own throat's health. She's worrying about everything.

I say all that only to illustrate that for Dusty, looking for a song must be a mission of encyclopaedic complication. Any song has to accord to so many demands. I have to say, she is a brilliant chooser.

"I'm a great believer in sheer volume and ploughing through things until you find the ones you want. It's just a matter of numbers. You're going to find something sooner or later."

Chronology and the passage of the nineteen sixties will bring up the subject of the songs Dusty DIDN'T write. Suffice at the moment to concentrate on the songs and the writers she DID choose for Dusty sings songs as though she DID write them. She knows them intimately, backwards, shaking a song like a terrier with a rat, until she's beaten it into submission. By the time Dusty's finished with a song, although she's inhabited it totally, she has also consumed it and it becomes - for her, not for us - an empty shell, of no further interest for she's already onto the next. What she has striven to find out becomes the knowledge she uses to go further. Yesterday's ends become tomorrow's means. Like a mountaineer, a foothold gained is one to be used. If there's a word for a song-a-maniac, please, somebody, tell me because Dusty's one.

"I was out on the road and I was doing NEEDLES AND PINS before THE SEARCHERS did it and things like that ... I would do lots of things that I heard in The States that weren't famous here and so I had a pretty, even then, fairly eclectic taste but because I was so convinced of what I was singing, it worked with the audiences. Bunny Lewis (Manager of THE MUDLARKS) told me, 'You have to make up your mind what you wanna sing,' which was the beginning of my realising that people need to pigeon-hole you ... All the early recordings, some songs were brought to me ... But basically I've found the songs and if I could sing 'em, that was right. It didn't matter if it was something from the seventeenth century or something from the Amazon ... on some of the albums ... Maybe that's why they didn't sell as well as they might have done, 'cos I insisted on putting oddities in!"

Dusty has said, though I choose whimsically to utterly disbelieve her, that when she first hears a song she doesn't listen to lyrics.

"I don't want to disappoint anyone but ... Anything that ever comes out as being affecting lyrically is constantly amazing to me because I'm much more interested in where the notes are."

"Everything depends on the music. Everything depends on the songs. If there aren't the songs there, I can't sing them."

For Dusty, America was a motherland for song-mining.

"I swiped anything that I heard from the States that wasn't going to be released here. That's the truth of it but then we all did. Cilla did it, the Beatles did it, we all did it ... But in those days, I actually did sort of sound fairly daring for a white singer. I knew that if Carole King wrote it, I was going to be able to sing it right. And some early Bacharach stuff. I mean, my voice certainly wasn't such a good marriage to Bacharach music as Dionne Warwick's was. But there were certain songs by Bacharach and David that were totally right. Like I JUST DON'T KNOW WHAT TO DO WITH MYSELF, things like that that were ..."

The story Dusty tells of how she got hold of THAT song, makes Sir Walter Raleigh's finding the potato in America pale with lack of daring.

"I JUST DON'T KNOW WHAT TO DO WITH MYSELF was

Tommy Hunt and I hadn't heard that record until Burt Bacharach played it for me and (when) I flew over to have dinner with him. I was at the Liverpool Empire and I remember leaving there and catching a 'plane on Sunday and having dinner with Burt Bacharach on the Sunday night and we went to his apartment, he played me that song ... I was crazy about THIS EMPTY PLACE which was the 'A' side of DION's record. When he played it to me, he said, 'Hear the other side' and that's how WISHIN' AND HOPIN' came about. So, it was a very productive trip. I remember exactly where we ate. A place called Dawson's Pub, probably not there anymore. It's on Third ... Yeah. He was really handsome. Still is."

Dusty was back on stage at the Liverpool Empire on Monday night.

"The one writer who gave me more pleasure to sing was Carole King. Somehow, her songs were like slipping on a glove. So intensely melodic there was this sweetness to them. But also they were soulful in their way and they were GREAT pop songs. I hardly know her. I met her once when she was probably eighteen and she blushed and so did I. She'd no idea how much I admired her and she was just this sort of little person who was then married to Gerry Goffin and was turning out these great pop songs ... It was like a rabbit warren in the Brill Building (In New York City) and all these writers in there churning this stuff out and she used to make such great demos that I collected them ... I used to copy them slavishly because you couldn't mess with them. You might be able to make it (a song) bigger or something, but you couldn't better it. I mean, I swiped SOME OF YOUR LOVIN' for that very reason. It was the most comfortable of songs to sing and it was the only record I've ever made that I brought home and played fourteen times in a row. I spent ages getting that muddy piano sound. They were going, 'It's not clear! It's not clear!' and I went, 'I don't WANT it to be clear. Take all the treble off ... Keep the pedal down, let all the notes all roll into each other. That's the way it's SUPPOSED to sound!' I was so ecstatically proud of it and it was, in hindsight, it truly was light years ahead of its time as a recording. And it was THAT record that got me (later) the Atlantic deal. She (Carole) didn't really want anyone to do GOIN' BACK, which was a song that touched

me to a certain extent. She really wanted to do it herself and, apparently, has gone down as saying that I'm the only other person that's ever done it that made it worthwhile. Which, coming from her, I just think is the best. What could be better than that?"

YOU DON'T HAVE TO SAY YOU LOVE ME turned out to be her biggest hit single. 1966. It was in the days when there were still Song Festivals; not vacuous, lowest common denominator Eurovisions but proper song festivals.

"YOU DON'T HAVE TO SAY YOU LOVE ME I heard at the San Remo song festival when it was sung, and written, by a guy called Peno de Nagio and I went crazy for the song. I brought back a record of it and sat on it for a year and then it seemed time to find an English lyric for it, desperately hoping someone else didn't do it. So, actually, I asked Vicki (Wickham) if she could put some words to it and she and Simon Napier-Bell - I think they wrote it in the back of a taxi or something. I just knew it was time for a big Italian type ballad and it was such a strong, strong tune. It really was. I can make a much better record of it now ... the sound would be much better ... But it worked."

And on the way, there were certain songs that got away. Like the fisherman who ALMOST caught the big one, Dusty still remembers the ones that got away ...

"I remember Valerie Simpson and Nicky Ashford in New York (The Brill Building) and ... obviously, I needed some material and they played me ... I went to their flat and sat there and they played AIN'T NO MOUNTAIN HIGH ENOUGH on the piano ... I just went mad for it and they said, 'Well, Dusty we have to tell you something ... We have to give this to Motown and if they accept it ... But if they don't, you can have it ... And the rest is awful history! I'd have killed for that song. It was everything I wanted in a song."

And other songs, however famous they've been made by another singer, can be given extra depth, extra significance, a whole new dimension by being cleverly and cannily chosen.

"TWENTY FOUR HOURS FROM TULSA ... Yeah, that was one of the first times a woman took a song that was essentially male and by singing virtually the same words, it became a different song. Now (adays) it would be nothing but then, it was

basically ... if you turned it around and a woman sang it, it was driving of into the night and being picked up at some gas station and ... this, that and the other ... and it was actually quite outre. There are songs you can do that way which because of the sound of a voice or an approach and being female, almost makes it a different song, lyrically ... It still gives it ... you still have the same intensity in the music."

Having conquered Britain and Europe, Dusty's attention was beginning to be wrested by the ever present call of her own wild frontier. America was in her blood.

In 1966 she proclaimed: *" Things are very dull for me in America. I don't agree with the way my career is being handled in the States. I think they (Mercury) are issuing the wrong stuff and I don't think I was given the right material when I recorded there."*

She was still going over regularly to promote her product.

"I had never played in the States for any length of time. I would come over and do spots on the Ed Sullivan Show and it was always the image of whatever single I had out at the time. So much of my image had been intermittent with those singles. You know, a little bit of WISHIN' AND HOPIN' here, a little bit of YOU DON'T HAVE TO SAY YOU LOVE ME there. I had no real broad range image. It was just sort of blonde beehive and miniskirts, waving her arms around ..."

In New York in 1966, she performed somewhat unhappily at Basin Street East, essentially a Jazz venue, not at all the sort of place she ought to have been playing. Dusty seemed still to be fighting all her own battles. Lots of men about, I'm sure but never when she needed them, when any-sex reinforcements would have been nice. On the bill with her at Basin Street East was Buddy Rich.

"What a bastard! He was the arsehole of the world. I went to ask him if I could have his band for half an hour's rehearsal - because I was headlining and I was expected to sing my hits like WISHIN' AND HOPIN' that his band had never even heard - He had his legs up on the desk and he said: 'You fuckin' broad! Who do you think you fuckin' ARE, bitch?' So, I punched him in the face."

By early 1967, Dusty's career found her earning a fabled

and much-advertised £1000 a night. Her shows, such as the one at the TALK OF THE TOWN where she tap-danced dressed as a Shirley Temple look-alike made front page news even in the respectable papers. Her wardrobe was much reported on, Marcelle Bernstein pointing out that her clothes were by Darnell of London - is that like Charnel of Paris? - and that her famous shimmering beaded dresses weighed up to thirty pounds each and cost £800. Now that was a lot of money then. I left university in 1968 and found a job with The British Council. As a graduate in a quasi-diplomatic environment I was earning nine hundred and something pounds a year. But, like Dusty spending as much on a frock - and good luck to her - as I earned in a year, I didn't like my life a whole lot either.

"It's rather difficult to know in which direction to go. I wouldn't like to be working in this business in twenty years time doing what I am doing now ... I'd be forty seven and who wants to be singing at forty seven? By then I hope I will have a settled mind."

Singing at forty seven? God forbid! And, in the same year, she said to Penny Valentine in DISC:

"What upsets me most at the moment in this business is that I'm moving into a cabaret bag. It's nice but the cabaret league isn't for me. What direction can I go in? I always wanted to be an actress but it's pretty unlucrative unless you can break into films. I'm just groping and wandering. All I know is that I have a distinctive voice I don't particularly like listening to."

CHAPTER NINE

Questions, questions ...

1967 saw the release of I'LL TRY ANYTHING, GIVE ME TIME and WHAT'S IT GONNA BE? as singles and the appositely entitled WHERE AM I GOING? as the November released album. As she asked directly of her interviewer, the entirely sympathetic and 'pretty deep-thinking' Penny Valentine, *'What direction can I go in?'* Whither indeed?

WHERE AM I GOING? entered the British chart at number 40 and stayed only for a week.

"That's really upset me because I'd worked hard on it. You can't keep thinking of chart success - you get past that. Of course it's important to have records in the charts as long as you can -it's very good for morale for one thing. But you can't make it the centre of everything."

She had worked hard on it and the battling didn't stop when it was finished. She was refused even a co-production credit on the album and so she insisted that NO ONE received credit.

As Bette Davis once said, 'Fasten your seat belts ...'

Time and Mary O'Brien and the woman called Dusty weren't on Dusty Springfield's side. The years of anyone's twenties are like a jelly. People's selves aren't properly identifiable at twenty one. One's twenties are a process of throwing away the least useful of what the teens have erupted and applying real life to the rest. At the beginning of that decade you're still swimming, still struggling. By the end, you're usually caught, trapped like a fly in amber. Thirty IS truly a dangerous age. The jelly is set. Its approach can upset even the most set in their ways and threaten to make runny jelly once again of anyone's life. Runny jelly looking for a mould.

Youth television had always loved the younger, bubbly, Queen-of-the-Mods Dusty. As she grew older and gained increasing musical respect, grown-up television also claimed her for their audience. Dusty made four television series post-1966. I can say hand-on-heart that personally I've never seen their equal since Tom Jones made a very under-rated series some two years ago.

The format was simple. Dusty and guests. Some remarkable guests. Dusty calls them, with wistful understatement 'a pretty eclectic mix'.

"I had all the musical say. The guests were ... It was what agent could get his client on whatever show was important to be on at that time. So, I mean, that's obviously why Woody Allen was on it because it was very early days for him and probably somebody said, 'There's this show ...' You know how they get lists of shows that you ought to be on. And it was live. So, um ... well, some of the guests were live. But I don't know ... I had very little to do with the guests basically. I mean, I was probably just trying to remember the words for the next song ... They're all a blur because there was so much going on ... I just remember the noise. I remember testing myself and going and standing by Marshall and just enjoying the fact that the BBC sound engineers were going totally spare. They didn't know what to do and I said, 'What the hell'. They'd go, 'Oh, the needle's going in the red. You can't do that' and I just said, 'Turn it up, turn it up', I was just testing myself to see where my threshold of pain was for sound. It was wonderful ... I wish I knew what show that was because there were four years of them. They get a bit jumbled up."

The range her guests covered was the acme of the gamut of contemporary writing and performing talent across the spectrum of style. And in turn, Dusty was a guests on other performer's specials. From Bacharach to Hendrix. On Bacharach's show she sang A HOUSE IS NOT A HOME.

"Was there a series of the Burt Bacharach show? Maybe it was just a special. It was definitely tuned for the States otherwise they wouldn't have had Juliet Prowse on it. I swear it was CBS because CBS at that time was making an awful lot of stuff in England out at either Shepperton or Elstree, Maybe Shepperton, I don't know, because the budgets ... they could keep them down so much. They'd get English dancers and English singers. I swear Liberace was CBS ... I told him (Bacharach) there are places where the singing's great and the hair's terrible and places where the hair's great but the singing's terrible. Sorry. You can't have both! Actually, it was quite hard to do ... took courage because it was extremely high and because I was in awe of him and because I couldn't hear the backing very well. Initially, I was just singing it with him at the piano. There's some stuff on the old BBC shows, a track called POOR WAYFARING STRANGER which is one on of them that I think is very touching and on another there's MY LAGAN LOVE. It's on one of the shows ... I actually sat on the floor and cried when I saw it a few months back. The voice was so pure and there was such courage in doing it out of the blue and then singing NOWHERE TO RUN immediately afterwards which I kind of like the idea of doing ... I must admit I probably was the only singer who could do that at that time in this country, suddenly switch gears like that."

On one of her own shows, Dusty sang with Jimi Hendrix and sadly all this work was in the days way before home video recorders or even sound cassettes. Now, any artist could have a tape of their work immediately, audio or visual. Then, you were lucky to go home from the studio with anything to play after a hard day's work.

"That I remember ... I mean, God knows what it was really like but I remember the occasion and the thrill of it. But, I mean, in hindsight, I don't know what it was like and I would love to know what it was like. I would love to hear that piece. I know it was MOCKINGBIRD - I think it was MOCKINGBIRD. But how it came out, I've no idea because everything was so rushed. You know, I spent my life, practically ... if the guest was on, I was probably trying to change and run to the sound booth at the same time screaming at the sound engineer to either let me hear

something or to remember to put the guitar up in the next number or something ... You know, I used to make charts up for them. In the time I was supposed to get ready before the show, I spent most of my time in the sound booth trying to get some sounds out. I'm sure I drove them absolutely bonkers ... I thought he (Hendrix) was so great and ... just being with that sound. I loved that sound. Just the idea of doing a duet with him was hysterical. That and doing - partly terrified of it but also the other part - I've never been so frightened as the one time on, doing RIVER DEEP MOUNTAIN HIGH. I think it was that or PROUD MARY. PROUD MARY maybe, with Tina. We had to run up those steps. I swear it was at Rediffusion and I couldn't hear myself think, she was singing so loudly. She and Patti, Patti Labelle. The vibrations coming out of that woman are so loud, you actually can't hear. You know, you're singing 'cos you can feel the strain but you actually can't hear the noise. I think it was probably like that with Jimi Hendrix. I've no recollection of any sounds coming out because there was probably so much sound coming out of the amps. I love sheer decibel level for the hell of it for about ten minutes and then I have to leave because I'm deaf."

As 1967 melted into 1968, I imagine that Dusty's life was beginning to ride a rockier road. The title of her 1968 album DUSTY ... DEFINITELY gives the impression that she is beginning to gird herself for a quantum leap away from the treadmill that she perceived life in England had become.

"I'm trapped more by commitments than anything else. But I'm very puzzled about where to go. I'm rapidly approaching the stage where I can't do more than about eight appearances here a year because there isn't the work that pays the kind of money I need. I can work every workingmen's club in the North but they wouldn't want me back next year. I have to spread it out, make myself desirable. It just doesn't do to be around too much."

Once again, in THE OBSERVER interview, Dusty wonders plaintively:

"I don't think I want to go on what I am doing for another five years. I'd be standing still. There are films, bigger things in the world."

By 1968, Dusty and Vic Billings had parted company. *"We decided we'd done as much for each other as we could,"* she announced somewhat peremptorily to Marcelle Bernstein. Dusty also told THE OBSERVER that at the moment she couldn't afford another manager, a puzzling remark when most putative managers of a star the size of Dusty Springfield would have cheerfully worked on a commission, commissions being tax deductible as a legitimate expense as far as income is concerned. I.E. The tax man pays for management.

The Dusty Springfield who stares rather hollowly out from 1968 pictures is a phenomenon who is beginning to sense that she is becoming trapped, a bird in an admittedly gilded cage but a cage nevertheless.

"At most there is three months' work for me in Britain and that's why I have to look elsewhere."

The horizons over which she was casting her eye lay indubitably westward. The direction alone presented an escape from the trap for the feeling of being trapped was niggling her.

"Really, I'm terribly upset if people think I'm neglecting them. If it gets printed that you are going to the States for a few weeks then people think you're going forever but it's just not true. I want to divide my time to please everybody."

And that was the problem. She was trying to please too many people and not herself. It's what they forget to tell you at Catholic schools. They tell you about selfishness the sin and selflessness the virtue. What they don't tell you is that if you're not occasionally selfish, you won't accumulate or retain the necessary strength in order to be selfless.

Pat Rhodes explained how much Dusty was influenced by her friends, especially new friends. She is eager to please, eager to show that she is likeable, lovable. The proclivity is symptomatic of her overall personality which wants more than anything to give out as much love in return for getting as much back as she can ... Trouble is, too, that you can control the love you give, but not the love you expect to get.

That ol' devil love again.

Dusty had few very close friends. The ones she had were very influential. Her flatmate at the time, Californian singer-songwriter Norman Tanega enlarged upon Dusty's life and, one presumes, state of mind:

"I can't stand to see anybody caught up in a world that inhibits them so much."

But it was the only world that Dusty knew, Norma ...

"It did feel like knocking my head against the wall. You start telling yourself these dark thoughts that seem very real, that maybe your time has passed. Then the panic comes on another level and you start saying to yourself, 'If you don't do this, what do you do? Because you don't know how to do anything else, you pitiful creature. All you know how to do is what you've done for years. You wouldn't know how to do an ordinary job. You'd die out there."

Lucy O'Brien in her book DUSTY quotes Dusty further:

"My feeling was that I had run out of things to do in Britain. I didn't want to get bored or be pinned down to summer seasons or the cabaret circuit. THE SPRINGFIELDS got out before people got tired of it. I could sense the rot setting in."

Though the guardian angels have once or twice been at lunch when Dusty needed them, in 1968 someone somewhere answered her unspoken call for a compass. Whoever it was sent a man from Atlantic records. A very nice man.

"Ahmet (Ertegun) was just over having a cup of tea with Goldie and the Gingerbreads. We all used to live in Bayswater in the same building - not Ahmet but Goldie and the Gingerbreads and Leapy Lee and Kenny Everett - or maybe Kenny came later, I don't remember the chronology of it. But I do remember it was our own little Brill Building and Ahmet was just there and so I played him SOME OF YOUR LOVIN' and he said, 'If you ever get free of your obligations elsewhere, come to Atlantic'. So I did. I was free in the States but I wasn't free here. So I went to Atlantic and I suppose it just came up as a good idea. I'm quite sure I didn't broach it. I'm sure it was them. I don't actually remember. But I was so pleased ... It was like somebody, as they say, validated and, actually, someone said, 'Yes, I get it'. You know?"

Dusty had often, previously, voiced her dis-satisfaction with the way her recorded material was handled in America. If fairness is to remain unimpeached, it has to be pointed out that

Dusty was NOT an American artist, therefore US record companies could hardly be blamed in those very early days for not knowing how to structure their role in a totally unstructured career situation. Dusty was British. She came west only occasionally. Perhaps, dare I say, the American aristomusicos were either a bit scared of her or they were more than a little wary of her being unable or unwilling to sustain their greater interest and investment in her? In short, were they not content to reaping whatever rewards they could from her hit single artist status? After all, they didn't make the records, they merely issued them. Dusty realised this, in part.

"I had cracked it (America) on an intermittent level ... After all, I ONLY WANT TO BE WITH YOU was a hit, WISHIN' AND HOPIN' was a hit, umm ... THE LOOK OF LOVE, YOU DON'T HAVE TO SAY YOU LOVE ME. I'd had quite a few hits but I was never there to take advantage of it. I mean I'd sort of be there to promote and then disappear off again and I just decided that I wanted to spend more time there. And after all, it was sixty three to sixty nine ... Six years was a long time to be sort of functioning at a very high profile level and I ... as I said, I'm fairly intuitive and ... there wasn't anywhere else I could go ... This (Britain) is a small country. So yes, it was partly sort of wanderlust which I will always have. I look at planes flying over and wish I was on them."

Flying into the maw of mainline, mainstream American music industry circles hardly implied functioning at anything less than a high profile level. But be that as it may ... She has no need to justify herself. Suffice to say that Dusty wanted to go.

Signing with Atlantic meant that Dusty was handing over the control of the making of her records to a new company. Future product would be made in America, budgeted in America and overseen in America by Americans, by strong American men who were MORE expert in both the art and politics of a more established record industry than Dusty.

Besides her ear being whispered into by her immediate friends, Dusty was, naturally, hugely flattered by Atlantic's interest, intrigued by the fresh, new prospects and proud, garnering a huge satisfaction that she was rated, 'validated' as she put it, by those she deemed worthy of her respect.

In 1968, Dusty once again set out for America, a tourist for the last time. I believe she went to Memphis more as a stateless asylum-seeker, casting herself adrift from her homeland, the cradle of her life so far.

"I'd like to make it clear that I'm not dis-satisfied with things here (in Britain) - only Phillips in America. The Atlantic deal is no reflection at all on Johnny Franz or any other people at Philips in Britain."

Them's easy words to say but to the vulnerable parent company they could have appeared like bullets. Biting them was tough. It must have been with somewhat gritted teeth that Phillips faced the future as Dusty's record company who would no longer be responsible for the making of her records; that they in their turn were now only to be licensees.

CHAPTER TEN

Is that Memphis...
Memphis Tenessee?

"When Jerry said we were going to do Dusty, I went out and bought the last four Dusty albums that had come out on Mercury and I knew every key she sang in, I knew her intervals, I knew pretty much where she was coming from. Also I knew that in spite of her being accepted as a ballad chanteuse in the American market, she was an astute jazz singer with incredible pitch so that when we went into Memphis I was armed. I knew where she could go or where she would come from. I was prepared."

Oh, yeah? Thus spoke Tom Dowd.

If he really did do all this arming himself, how much preparation had Jerry Wexler done, how much homework had Arif Mardin done and what research must have been churning round in the corporate bowels of Atlantic records? Phew! As the bumpy road sign warns wary motorists, there were definitely MEN AT WORK in Memphis.

I wonder if they had taken into account that they were about to be enjoined by a very British lady, one who was shy to the point of chronic, wary to the point of suspicion, cautious to the point of trepidation and not the sort who would be swayed, cajoled, persuaded or entreated by anything less than total understanding and forbearance approaching the saintly.

For once, Dusty wasn't in charge. Seems she hadn't REALLY thought about that one. These Memphis men were team players, it seems. Dusty had never played anything but the recording business version of singles tennis; the pro-am football team benches was one place she'd never sat.

She went into Memphis still playing her singles tennis and she was doing so without a back-up. She was running for her own balls. She had many coaches but no manager, a glaring omission especially in America where she needed it badly, a management geared to the up-coming era of the Joni Mitchells, the Carole Kings, the Carly Simons ... Someone like Peter Asher? Someone new, dynamic, thrusting, adventurous, someone with their fingers on the pulse of the up-coming seventies when rock music would come of age.

Instead, Dusty had ... no one or, at least, no one whom she could publicly acknowledge as a manager. In Britain, she was less one Vic Billings. Marcelle Bernstein reported that Dusty owed Vic £20,000 (that's almost a quarter of a million in today's ready folding stuff) for two years of a contract from which he was ousted. Why? Why, for heaven's sake? Unaccountably, Dusty was trying to do everything herself.

Pat Rhodes thinks she was utterly exhausted, couldn't see the wood for the trees and wanted, basically, to get out, to escape, to lie low. No wonder. Business, schedules, shopping, recording, choosing songs and ... and England was beginning to get under her skin, beginning to get to her in more personal ways.

In the days of the Hollywood Studios, the 'Dusty problem' would have been taken care of. Had Dusty been a pet of a huge record monolith, a 'good' girl with the 'right' smart Mayfair management, she would have been fine. But she was on her own. She was too quirky to be anything's pet, too independent to be the outpost of anyone's empire, too sensitive to be anyone's bondswoman before immediately escaping.

It was probably cumulative word of mouth that made Dusty start to be considered fair game and she was to find out that the Fleet Street pack are never out for a run. They need blood. They might not print the blood but they want to see it; launder it a bit, perhaps. Certainly store it.

Fleet Street, wherever it works, is like a blood bank for unwilling depositors and the interest they exact for holding the bonds of people's secrets is mortal. The gutter press had already stepped off the pavement by the late sixties but some of them did it so elegantly, so respectably, in Gucci shoes ... journalism was still so unbespattered.

"I have been extremely hurt by people saying things about me. I have a certain pride in myself as a woman and it upsets my femininity. And because I don't float round from premiere to premiere, I've been criticised. They say you're either a prostitute or a lesbian, so if you're neither where are you? You can't be in the middle, in people's minds. I've done nothing wrong and I refuse to invent a relationship to appease them."

These are the words of a lady protesting, a lady whose dignity has been ruffled by 'people' (journalists) asking the hitherto unaskable question although quite what prostitution had to do with the matter in hand, I'm not sure. Dusty's are also the words of someone who clearly hasn't worked out their reply to the question she should have been expecting and who clearly SHOULD have not only worked out one answer but several and learned them verbatim. The flustered puppeteer was caught, as the canvas blew away from the front of the tent show, with her hands up the puppet's bottom. People were beginning to notice.

Dusty Springfield, as a construct, had been made to sport, if required, a consort, a respectful, two-paces-behind but nevertheless-always-there consort. She didn't have one. There was no consort in sight. People were bound to ask. It was the one thing in the manufacture of Miss ... Dusty ... Springfield that hadn't really been thought of.

The power of rumour has always amazed me. The sheer force of gossip and the speed and intensity at which it spreads, like a forest fire fanned by a mistral, is incredible. Even now, twenty five years on, I mention casually to friends and acquaintances that I have turned my attention to writing about the work of Dusty Springfield and out comes - from whomsoever I meet - a complete dossier, a personality catalogue, friends of friends who once worked with her, danced in her show, stood next to her at READY STEADY GO!, know someone who went out with her, saw her on an aeroplane, at a tennis match ...

I only have to open my window and call than any passer-by will tell me all about Dusty Springfield. They seem to know where she is, what she's doing, who she's doing it with ... And they seem to have their information spot on! How? I don't know this stuff. HOW DO THEY KNOW?

It's like when we sit around and cheerfully toss back and forth the career, liquidity, behaviour and morality of someone who is SO familiar to us, we THINK we know them well enough to PRESUME to talk about them behind their backs in intimate detail. If we could hear ourselves doing it, perhaps we might not but we ALL do it. I'm sure Dusty does it just as much as she herself is the subject of other people's idle attention. So, Dusty's contemporarily quoted words to Marcelle Bernstein amaze me by their sheer naivety. They also make me sad for her apparent innocence.

"The authority I have in my job can carry through to my private life. If somebody's personality is weaker than mine, I take over. Or else I'm so frightened of this happening that I don't act naturally at all. It's very difficult to be a completely natural woman in the company of a man; few can manage an attitude between, 'My God! It's you!' and 'Who are you, anyway?'. The responsibility of being - for want of a better word - a star means I feel almost masculine. It's like being a husband - I've got to pay the bills. I find it alienates men. I want to get married but I dislike failure in anything. To enter into marriage, to want to succeed and have it fail is to me the dread failure of all. It's the failure of myself as a human being."

I mean ... Puhleeze! The Queen did it, Dust. Princess Margaret, Princess Anne, Grace Kelly did it ... So have thousands of powerful women more celebrated than their spouses. Do you really think they get asked, 'Excuse me, ma'am, would your graciousness be interested in the pork sword tonight?'

I read Dusty's words in sheer disbelief that someone could be so isolated from the current of show business gossip, tittle tattle, rumour and innuendo that they don't know when, at worst, to shut up or, at best, to say nothing or, the very best, to lie. Why NOT invent something?

Whoever was advising her was doing a pretty bad job of bearding Dusty or a pretty good job of self-outing as we would say in these post-Gay Lib days. Pre-Gay Lib, Ms. Bernstein's feature was as close as 'outing' got, especially in responsible, respectable, respectful journalism as sported in THE OBSERVER.

"'All the orange things and all the toys in the flat are Dusty's,' remarks Norma. It was she who decorated the £20,000 house Dusty is moving into near Campden Hill Square, Kensington. (Why not give the postcode too?) Norma spent over £6000 on the conversion and every fitting is properly star-like: vast sunken bath is reflected in amber glass, the double bed (are there no other beds?) looks quadruple at least and the fridge wouldn't be out of place at the Savoy. But their house-keeping is somewhat erratic: when they decide to have bacon and eggs at three in the morning, they ring their local cab service to bring the bacon. And the 'phone bill must be impressive - to settle an argument about whether Forest Lawn is the name of a Californian tennis court or a cemetery, they ring a friend in Los Angeles to find out."

In these words, Ms. Bernstein is not describing the antics of the sixth form at St. Trinians nor the cavorting of two female teenage Cliff Richard fans in a pink-flounced bedroom. Ms. Bernstein is completing the unfinished portrait to which she has previously drawn our attention, the portrait which Norma Tanega has done of Dusty. Did Norma ever complete the picture, I wonder?

However, for all of those who've been desperate to know for all these years, I can most definitely proclaim without a shadow of a doubt that, Ladies and Gentlemen, Miss ... Dusty ... Springfield is NOT a lesbian for, and let's not forget it, MISS DUSTY SPRINGFIELD ONLY EXISTS as Marcelle Bernstein describes the phenomenon in the final paragraphs of her 1968 article:

"And she really seems to grow taller, slimmer before the footlights. It's not just long false nails that extend her fingers but the almost-love, the rapport between watchers and watched, audience and star. Her hands become expressive and supple, emphasising the movements of her body, the timbre of her voice as she stands in a glitter of excitement and diamante".

Then it's over and she bows low, one hand in the spotlight:

she twists her wrist and the fingers flicker, caught on the applause."

Just who IS the lesbian is not for me to say and for others to wait for confirmation. But don't hold the space or your breath. No one can ever accurately finish Norma's painting.

CHAPTER ELEVEN

"The receipt's in the bag ...
If you want to change it, that is."
"Oh. thanks. no. Absolutely not ...
It's, er, perfect."

The album, DUSTY IN MEMPHIS, the present her future had given her, was released in April 1969.

I don't feel her state of mind was on her side during these recordings which were obviously punctuated by several trans-atlantic trips to fulfil contractual obligations. Furthermore, the album could just have easily and more accurately been entitled TRACKS IN MEMPHIS, DUSTY IN NEW YORK.

"I'd been there (Memphis) before but just for television things. I mean, I wasn't really aware of Memphis because you just go to a studio. Besides, most of Memphis (the album) was made ... We cut the tracks in Memphis but most of it was done in New York. I hate to debunk that but ... It was great, you know what Jerry Wexler's like. Keep 'em laughing ... Great good humour."

But behind the jollity ...

"I felt very uptight about it ... exposed all of a sudden. But I sort of grew up as the album progressed. Working this way forces you to be creative."

Her omnipresent self-criticism and the attendant self-deprecation came marching to the fore. She was, after all, being recorded by Aretha Franklin's team.

"Jerry's (Wexler) gone into print saying I was the most insecure singer he has come across. What he didn't realise was how intimidated I was. Because they were telling stories, talking about 'Aretha' and I'm going, 'What am I DOING on this label? WHY are they recording ME?' That showed in the time it took to get vocal performances out of me. Because if there's one thing that inhibits good singing it's fear or allowing the natural critic in me to criticise a note before it even left my throat which destroys the flow of anything. I don't think they understood how intimidated I was so it probably came out as scowls and fear and grumbling ..."

To Sharon Davis, she explained:

"I got destroyed when someone said, 'Stand there. That's where Aretha stood' or 'Stand there. That's where Percy Sledge sang WHEN A MAN LOVES A WOMAN'. I became paralysed by the ghosts of the studio! I knew that I could sing the songs well enough but it brought pangs of insecurity ... that I didn't deserve to be there. I just knew that Aretha's drummer was going to say, 'Well ain't SHE a piece o' shit'. It's the most deflating thing you can say to me that someone I adore and worship actually stood there and probably delivered an effortless performance while I'm slogging away trying to get it right. They meant well but they didn't realise what they were doing ... It's funny but I hated those sessions but the albums do say everything about the patience those guys had. They worked with me until they got it out of me. Probably the irony of those whole sessions was that I was so crippled with laryngitis they could only record me two or three words at a time. Yet there are notes on the album that I've never sung again. They're so HIGH. I'd be revving up and I'd just go for it. When I didn't make it, I'd do it again until I did. It was rough!"

Dusty clearly remembered the efforts she made to sing.

"I think the highest and most sure I've ever sung is some of the fades on some of the Memphis songs. They're pretty ... they're stratospheric! I've never hit them again. I don't know how I did it. I just loved the songs so much that I'd probably take a ... stand about ten yards from the mike and run up to it, come out with it. Those songs are ... they just have tremendous atmosphere and they have a great quality. So, I suppose, yeah

... But only the fades. I always like the fades on things so I get an enormous sense of relief when we get to the fade which takes the anxiety out of it, which means I can sing higher. It's daft, isn't it? They should put the fade first. By the time we got to the end, the beginning would be terrific!"

Dusty found the recording techniques initially very different to those to which she had become accustomed.

"At that point (the beginning) it was a lot more relaxed but they got a lot done at the same time which is how I'm told Nashville is. But they would come in and they would more or less clock in. It was like a house band and they would just sort of make it up, basically, which was quite something when we came to WINDMILLS OF YOUR MIND because they had never approached anything like that before. I didn't want to do that song. Jerry did and so I went along with it. But it caused absolute mayhem in the studio trying to get the chords right and it was I who slowed it down. Originally it was very much faster and I think I slowed it down so that it would be more organised. But they weren't used to doing that kind of thing but it was much more relaxed and we just sort of got as much done in a day as you could whereas in with not enough happening and it was ... Although Arif put the strings on afterwards but they still built it more and then did the vocals when I was more comfortable in New York. I can be really good and feel ... you know, everything flows and ... Try and match it the next night and it's not there. I mean I would like it always to be level and always to be there but it's not. It's not but hopefully the amount of work I do in the periods when I'm flying is worth it and then there's a bit of a quiet time ... Then it comes back again."

Dusty has always appeared torn in her own assessment of her MEMPHIS album.

"I didn't and probably still don't (feel euphoric). But what I see in hindsight - It's always in hindsight - I should never judge things at the time because I'm not objective ... The record has a real atmosphere and continuity to it. There are a couple of things that don't belong on it but unlike the other albums which were all over the place because I was doing the choosing, these (the MEMPHIS songs) were mutually chosen by Jerry and I - and Tom. And it showed, that there was real continuity to it and a

feeling ... The further I'm away from it, the better I think it is and I suppose it took me a long time to distance myself. This happens ... I'm no good at accepting praise at the time. I've become a lot less inwardly arrogant that I used to be in that I didn't SHOW my arrogance, but my INNER arrogance - 'It isn't good enough!' 'WHY do you say it's good?' 'It CAN'T be good because I say it's NOT good!' ... I'd be smiling and I'd say 'Thank you' but I couldn't take the praise then because the critic was functioning full time."

To Adam Sweeting, she said more succinctly on one of the days when she didn't like MEMPHIS too much:

"It's become rather an over-rated classic. It's not as if it's some magnificent work of art. It's a good record."

The world, however, had its own opinions. These can be fairly summed up by re-iterating Marcus Greil's review of MEMPHIS in the March 1969 edition of ROLLING STONE.

"With the single THE LOOK OF LOVE, Dusty seemed destined to join that crowd of big-bosomed, low-necked lady singers that play what Lenny Bruce called, 'The class rooms' and always encore with BORN FREE. It didn't happen and DUSTY IN MEMPHIS is the reason why ... Dusty is not a soul singer and she makes no effort to 'sound black' - rather she is singing songs that ordinarily would have been offered by their writers to black vocalists. Most of the songs have a great deal of depth while presenting extremely direct and simple statements about love. Unlike Aretha who takes possession of whatever she does, Dusty sings around her material, creating music that's evocative rather than overwhelming. Listening to this album will not change your life but it will add to it ..."

Dusty might not have liked MEMPHIS much at the time but it was money in the bank for later.

CHAPTER TWELVE

"I want to get out of London..."

In 1969, Dusty made A BRAND NEW ME with the same team. It came out in Britain in October 1970. It was called FROM DUSTY ... WITH LOVE. The American title was as apt as the British. Hello and Goodbye. The postcard home would have read, 'Glad you're not here!' By October 1970, London must have seemed a long way away, emotionally, romantically, artistically.

"... I was no longer having hits so rather than live on the past, I thought I'd try and start again. And, I had a certain amount of success with my album DUSTY IN MEMPHIS ..." She'd got that 'coming home' feeling again.

"There's something about America which seems to fit me. Things like waking up in the middle of the night and knowing you can walk around the block and buy food in a supermarket."

As we know, Dusty's remark applies firmly to Metropolitan America. The big cities. Eighty percent of America shuts down early, eats dinner early, goes to bed early, gets up early. MOST of America wasn't for our Dust, the nightbird. In MOST of America, if a dyed-blonde single woman was spotted by the local police department walking along Main Street she'd have been busted for soliciting however much she protested she was 'just looking for a supermarket, officer.'.

I suppose that to her and to everyone around her, Transatlantic Avenue must have all seemed a good avenue to head down.

"I was coming to the end of a fairly good run here (Britain). I'm a firm believer in sort of quitting before they fire you. It's just a matter of being one step ahead. I could see that the writing was on the wall in the same way THE SPRINGFIELDS knew THE BEATLES were coming along and stopped. We knew the time to stop and I knew that my run was coming to an end of the hype that it had been at the height it had been, the intensity ... and besides, I was in love with America since a kid. It was where I wanted to be."

Dusty chose to settle in California. It could have been New York but Dusty knew something of New York. She also had a new set of friends, tennis players and she seemed perfectly content to stay off the court herself and be photographed carrying other people's racquets. Gradually, like she was shopping for a whole new outfit in expensive shops on Rodeo Drive, she acquired a new look for her career structure.

"Was the grass greener? No. I was in California because that's where I had a manager at the time and it was one of those people that they take you out for a big breakfast - Dusty? Breakfast meetings? It's amazing what a change of air can do! - and then you can never get them on the 'phone. It's one of those situations when I was, you know, with Creative Artists and William Morris and all the right things and all I landed up doing was basically night club stuff."

Was it really a case of 'From the frying pan into the fire'?

"I did, actually, a lot of televisions but MOST of it was playing the Blue Room at the Roosevelt Hotel in new Orleans and the 'something' room at the Fairmont in San Francisco, the Persian Room at the Plaza and I had it all written and it was all quite slick and I suddenly realised I didn't like it very much but I was making a good living and that's what people did. That's what the outlets were for people. That's what singers did in the States at that time. They may still, I don't know."

She's right. That was it. Dinner Theatre was only just getting going. Jazz Clubs in the metropolis existed and a few music clubs. In Los Angeles there was Doug Weston's Troubadour. In New York there was the Bottom Line. Pat Rhodes confirms that Dusty does not work well in small rooms with cutlery and glasses clattering. She likes large, seated audiences in a theatrical context. Theatres are where she came from and they're what she knows. Touring in the states was never mooted and if it was, it never materialised. She now jokes about it.

"... Subsequently, I closed the Finsbury Park Empire ... I did! I closed a club in New York - The Bottom Line. What other theatre did I close? No, it was The Bottom Line that closed - it did. Maybe it was for renovations but it certainly wasn't there next time I went back. Grand Finale - that's it! Grand Finale and indeed it was. And there was one other place that closed the week after I'd closed it. So, I don't really know much about touring ..."

The immigrant Dusty hadn't remade her image. She hadn't sniffed the wind and sensed the change of season. I'm not at all sure that had she done so, she would have hacked it at that particular time of her life any differently. Dusty, perhaps goaded by a re-discovered Mary O'Brien, wanted for a change to be looked after, taken care of, cossetted, maybe even allowed to sleep for a year and wake up ...different.

The only 'different' she got was in terms of her own unreality. By 1970, Dusty was yet one step further removed from her control of Dusty Springfield. Sure, the Americans had come in and bought the image, the big blonde image. That's what they could sell. When they told her they could sell Dusty Springfield, there were being absolutely honest. They weren't interested in anything that existed underneath and if they were, they probably merely assumed that if THEY fed Dusty Springfield, SHE could feed who the hell else she'd brought along with her. Mary? Dusty?

And, although at her own insistence she never played anywhere in Las Vegas, it has to be said that the American cabaret circuit is VERY different from the (then) British circuit that always included Batley and all those Baileys!

"I knew I couldn't sing two shows in a night, seven nights a week. I'm no good at that. The best one was ... I did play (Lake) Tahoe and that was great, that was with THE SPINNERS and it was a very special week. For some reason, the entire place closed down for one night and it was only for, like, six nights so

basically we did two nights, or three nights, and then I had a day off and then did the other two or three nights. Which was ... I've no idea why it was, maybe it was a Shriners' evening or something like that but that was a lot of fun. That was my only experience of that but it was wonderful because it was with THE SPINNERS. They were wonderful ... ARE wonderful!"

Like the seamlessness which Dusty had picked up on and admired, even envied, about the Motown music she so loved, the rest of American show business she found to be just as seamless. Seamlessness is expected of you. You buy in, you have to have the necessary or they simply close your subscription. You have to supply no-cut, no-sew ready-made seamless ...

The only real experience that Dusty had had to fore-arm her was singing on shows like HULLABALLOO in the sixties.

" ... ten o'clock in the morning at the Hollywood Palace having to sing WISHIN' AND HOPIN' with a pianist who didn't know it. With Lucille Ball sitting on a chair and Fred Astaire going, 'Good! That's good!' You know, having the courage to actually ... and going, 'I've got to sing WISHIN' AND HOPIN' with the piano at ten in the morning and Lucille Ball is smiling at ME!'. You've just gotta have the guts to do it because they all do it."

I think I mentioned before that in Britain there isn't a Royal Academy for Performers and Singers so you just had to hack it. Of course, in America the performing arts are taken far more seriously because it's been acknowledged that they make a helluva lot of money; making money, in Britain it seems, is a dirty connotation. Better to subsidise, give them a grant ... Perhaps, but just HOW do Americans all get so damned good? Is it that there are five times many more population that Britain has and so whoever comes out on top is likely to be five times as good? Uh uh. Doubt it. And there are damn few subsidies over there!

" ... I did notice, the more I worked with people like that, you know ... with THE OSMONDS and Andy Williams, they were so incredibly professional and so organised with people, writers ... You know, writing this scene and that routine ... and they were great at mixing songs up, medleys and somebody would be singing one thing against somebody singing another and they

were really good at that. Like the people who used to write for Carol Burnett and all those people and the expectation was that you could do it, so you did and you did it well or you did it to the best of your ability ... The actual material may have been corny but it was well-crafted. I mean, that routine I do with Liberace and Phyllis Diller and Millie Martin, that was American written. I'm quite sure I was terrified but the expectation was - You can DO it so I did. And the nineteen forties musical thing with Englebert Humperdinck, Jonathan Winters. I thoroughly enjoyed that but I never got a chance to do that here; although we did it here it was for American television ... Over there they would incorporate a pop singer and you do a song, but then they wanted you to work with the rest of them, like a team and for this frantic four days you became a team and you became a team member and you learnt things and if they wanted you to mince around and do this, that or the other, you did it. Sometimes it didn't come off but most of the time I rose to the occasion because, while I was in awe of it, I suddenly realised I could do that and I wasn't on my own. There were always other people to watch out of the corner of your eye to do something. And you were working with people who knew how to duet properly or how to do ensemble work. How can you fail when you've got lots of voices around you who are all singing exactly the right thing? I mean, just working with THE OSMONDS ... they'd come out and they'd sing on a rehearsal and they'd sing perfectly and then they'd go back and do their schoolwork and then an hour later ... 'Boys! We need you.' They'd come out, do it perfectly, five perfect voices, close harmonies, perfect. Go back, do the algebra ... It was that kind of standard and you'd better live up to it ... It's there and it's right and it's high quality and it was wonderful to be a part of it, it really was compared to the chaos and lack of budget and trying to get things on here. It IS about money, I think and just having more to choose from. There's more overall-talented people because there are more people. It doesn't mean to say that great things and probably the most special things haven't come out of THIS country."

This is the myopic, shy girl, still without contact lenses, insecure, jittery, bag of nerves, the inadequate girl who was always comparing herself ... She must have thought she'd crashed the final year course at the School for Performing Arts in the FAME TV series.

"Here (in Britain) I think the ones that come through have done it in spite of circumstances because they have a very special talent or drive or anger... something. But there (in America) ... There was a ... I think it's just 'We've got a show to put on!' and everyone, for that time, they may be bitching in the background somewhere or other but everyone is there for that reason and there are lots of them and they will work to get that show out and the next week and the next week and the next week. They've got so many people to do it and, yes, they will shore you up. You go in there and there are fittings at, say, Warner Brothers or something at eight in the morning or half past seven in the morning and they are actually building costumes and the sequins are flying all over the place. I remember just walking in there and the thrill of watching the whole studio wardrobe department. It just doesn't exist anymore, but to listen to those people at that hour of the morning turning out this incredible stuff it was like ... I suppose the end of the old studio system. They were using film studio wardrobe people. Or just going into CBS wardrobe, everything was so - or appeared to be so - organised, which I really welcomed. They'll tell you you can do it and you're going to be all right. You don't feel as though you're moving mountains. They do it every week so while there's an expectation of you, you kind of know you CAN do it because everyone's doing it and you're lifted up by it and carried along by it. It's all funny as hell but it doesn't matter because it works and if you never see them again, it doesn't matter ... Who wants to? But for that four or five days that it takes to put that one hour special on, everything is working as smoothly as it possibly can and everyone's efforts are just on that and I really like that a whole lot."

Being part of a group ... Once again, America seemed to be assuaging Dusty's psychological requirements for her to work well. She didn't HAVE to be the boss ... She didn't have to constantly entertain that old niggling ghost identified by BBC television director Stanley Dorfman, the "... lack of faith in all the technicians who work with her. She seems to think they're not going to bother when in fact everyone's knocking themselves out. She doesn't want to leave anything in anyone else's hands, although the end is so rewarding."

Pat Rhodes, remembering her feelings from almost a quarter of a century ago, adds her own confirmation to the perspective. She felt something was not right about Dusty's move to America. Dusty asked her to accompany her, to make a new life in California but by that time Pat was married. Her husband's job and also the arrival of her baby son for once directed her priorities away from Dusty. Now, although she knows that remaining in Britain was a wise decision for herself, she also wishes she could have been in California for Dusty.

By the time BRAND NEW ME had been released in England and Dusty had done the requisite interviews, she seems to have been very conscious of having burned a bridge.

Penny Valentine had always given Dusty great interviews. Penny conveyed the essence of the BRAND NEW ME that Dusty Springfield apparently wanted understood.

"I burp like anyone else and I'm promiscuous. My affections are easily swayed and I can be very unfaithful. A lot of people say I'm bent and I've heard it so many times that I've almost learned to accept it ... I couldn't stand to be thought of as a big butch lady. But I know that I'm as perfectly capable of being swayed by a girl as a boy. More and more people feel that way and I don't see why I shouldn't ... Being a woman is very precious to me and that's probably why I could never get mixed up in a gay scene because it would be bound to undermine my sense of being a woman."

Well. That's tellin' em, Dust.

To Penny Valentine she added:

"D'you realise, what I've just said could put the final seal to my doom. I don't know, though. I might attract a whole new audience."

There's an apocryphal stage direction in playtexts which was supposed to have summarised the only option left to a character who'd just uttered an immortal yet clobberingly final line: EXIT STOUT PARTY.

Dusty has often been quoted as maintaining Peggy Lee to

be an icon, the artist whom she would most like to have been like.

"I had a fierce crush on Peggy Lee's voice. That's who I wanted to be. I wanted to be Peggy Lee."

This, to me, is a very strange ambition. Peggy Lee's life and career are well-documented. There were several VERY important things that either Dusty wasn't or didn't that Peggy was and did. Two VERY important ones were firstly writing songs and secondly, playing 'the class rooms' as well as the theatrical concerts. The 'class rooms' exist to enable artists, who so wanted, to play a decent sized auditorium where one existed. In middle America, you have to take what you can get and if you have to do it with a smallish band, you do it! Peggy did and the musicians from whom she could choose working bandmembers were legion and all from her own cultural backyard. What American musicians Dusty knew would have been mainly the ones who worked studios and many of them were already well-aware of the Boadicea of bassmen.

Peggy also wrote songs. Dusty had hardly even co-written although Chris White asserted in MUSIC WEEK that she part-wrote some of her sixties B-sides.

Whilst Dusty was associated with her brother Tom, she had not felt the need to write. Tom was the writer. Had Dusty attempted something, which I cannot believe she didn't even in the light of her feeling that she was not a natural songwriter, the likelihood of her showing it to or pushing it in the face of even the slightest criticism from Tom would have been minimal. She would have feared the possibility of rejection or scorn too much.

Pat Rhodes confirms there had been more than a flickering of interest at the end of the sixties. Dusty was, as could be expected, more than aware of the changing trend and had started to write.

"It really is an effort to be locked away in a room but maybe if I could discipline myself or work with someone else, then it might happen."

However, her interest was little encouraged by Norma Tanega, then her flatmate who herself was a singer and writer. Dusty was also being constantly flooded with other people's efforts. She recounts how PREACHER MAN came her way:

"... in the early days when we were trying to find music for the album (Memphis), Gerry Greenberg sent me that, SON OF A PREACHER MAN and JUST A LITTLE LOVIN' on a tape of about twenty songs and those were the two I picked out. Subsequently I went to Gerry's house in Little Neck or Great Neck or one of those Necks and we waded through songs for a week ... As far as feelings go, I'm apprehensive to a certain extent but as the songs get better and better that are coming in, I get more and more excited."

Surrounded by other people's creativity, it is amazing how easily one can slide one's own onto the back burner.

Dusty recorded SEE ALL HER FACES on which she managed to include a single production credit for herself although tied with Johnny Franz. Only five of the tracks were produced by the Wexler/Dowd/Mardin triumVIRate.

Finally, in 1973, CAMEO was released on ABC Records in the States, on Philips in Great Britain. Produced by yet another triumVIRate, Steve Barri, Dennis Lambert and Brian Potter, five of the songs on the album were by Lambert and Potter. Nice little earner. The album cover depicts a bleached out, line-drawn cartoonised likeness of an illusion of a once-upon-a-time phenomenon created by a stranger.

It might have been Dusty's voice but where had Dusty Springfield gone? There were to be only rare sightings for the next five long years.

CHAPTER THIRTEEN

California Sweet

Answer truthfully the following question:

Assuming you are financially independent, young and good-looking enough to enjoy it, would you like to go and live in Los Angeles? Answer, yes.

Now ask yourself:

Would you, being of sound mind, willingly go and live on top of an impending earthquake?

Er, yes. Do you see what I'm trying to get at it? The earthquake is the earthquake. See it as analogous to danger. The danger, basically, mattered to Dusty not a jot.

If five years seemed a long time to her fans, they must have been an eternity to Dusty. The first two or three years in America she summed up thus, in Lucy O'Brien's DUSTY and, it has to be said, in retrospect with a truckload of hindsight.

"A lot of work in America had been romanced (romanticised?) by the American Management. After all, they had all managed the best people. I should have followed my intuition though - my insides told me that it was wrong. They were pushing me towards nightclubs, the equivalent of what I was trying to get away from in England. I did intermittent albums and there was no continuity to anything."

The only continuity in her life can be glimpsed in the following utterance, through which one can almost touch the history of a being who, swathed in the protective envelope of a spotlight feels caressed and loved by strangers and yet who, forced back onto her own resources, is totally lost, dependent for love on making exhibitions of herself.

"Somewhere - you never know when - I crossed the line from heavy drinking into problem drinking. I was addicted to all sorts of things. So were many of us. I'm an addictive personality. A lot of us who went through the sixties went through a training period of being ravers. It was encouraged. The more you fell downstairs and indulged in lunatic behaviour, the more people said, 'Oh, she's a right card. Isn't she?' And, actually, it worked for a while ... I felt I was obsolete with a feeling of uselessness and depression."

Los Angeles itself began to pall after a while.

"Parts of this city (L.A.) are really naff. Parts are glamourous. I like the convenient aspects to it, things like the twenty four hour cleaners but I don't like the heat. And, musically, Americans have me pigeon-holed with that awful term 'blue-eyed soul singer'. They get frightened if you fling a lot of stuff at them, playing several different styles makes them nervous ..."

Funny. I thought she was afraid of being pigeon-holed as a cabaret artist, afraid of being pigeon-holed period?

In 1990, describing life in California to Chrissie Iley, Dusty encapsulated her situation:

"You have to adapt or die there (California) and I chose to get out because it would have killed me eventually. I just didn't know how to deal with the vacuousness."

She also, by implication, decided she wasn't going to adapt.

"I handle idleness very badly, so I really had to kick myself in the butt and get out of there."

However, on and off, it would take Dusty seventeen years and a couple of mock-escapes before she finally made it out. Between 1973 and 1977, it seems she played housewife.

"For as long as I can remember, I've been in love with the idea of California. It came first from the Hollywood Musicals I saw as a child and later through friends in the music business. I was determined to go and, once there, determined to be as Californian as possible. To adjust to that way of life, I did all the

things that Beverly Hills women do. You take care of your make-up, you go to lunch, you drink too much, you experiment with drugs, you shop, you make appointments, you develop a social circle. I would spend ages shopping for those enormously complicated recipes and cooking them very successfully and getting very fat. And I really hated it. It became so incredibly boring after a while. The fact is that I'm just not that kind of person. It was an attempt to fit in and it was so ... yuk, so superficial. I played the game ..."

Twenty years after deciding at school that she wouldn't play the game, Dusty found she'd fallen foul of the very thing her personality, character and career had ensured she would never had to do. It seemed she'd come a very little way.

"I thought that in order to put down roots, I had to buy a house. (Prior to the purchase she had lived in four different apartments) So I bought one on the (San Fernando) valley side of Laurel Canyon. It had a fantastic view, a big pool, all the gadgets. It was sort of nouveau riche. The trouble was that I was not very nouvelle and not very riche. I staggered around that house for a while trying to convince myself that I really belonged. But every time I looked at the burnt-up hillside, I felt terribly alien."

By her own account, she felt the constricting nature of the matriarchal environment.

"I began looking at these women and thinking, Christ ... What a load of bullshitters. I realised their lives didn't add up to anything, that they were a waste of time ... I dropped the cooking, I dropped the social life, I dropped the massage and I got back to work, to vocal lessons, to trying to get the pulse of the music scene."

In an interview with Peter Evans. Dusty sounds more as though she is unburdening herself on a doctor's couch rather than chatting professionally to a journalist.

"... when I started working here, something happened. My thinking musically was here, only I lost confidence in myself. I lost the ability to voice my opinions. I suddenly started thinking that maybe my views were amateur and empty. After all, I kept telling myself, 'This is Hollywood!'. I thought, 'What do I know?

This is the ultimate. This is where they made all those movies with Betty Grable and Don Ameche and Dan Dailey and Alice Faye. They must know more than I do. I floundered miserably. That was a low time. California can be a dangerous place to come to alone. It's a very strange country in many ways ... I'm a tough lady in many ways but my emotional stamina is not terrific. I'm inclined to get panicky. So when things started to go wrong, I got depressed and very lost for a couple of years ... The rest of the time since then has been sort of reconstructional - admitting how lost I was. Trying to do something about it. I wish I could tell you I've been painting or tap-dancing or growing potatoes in Idaho. I haven't. I've simply been destroying what was wrong with my life - as a woman, as a performer - and building on the debris. I grew up more last year (1977) than in the whole of the rest of my life put together ... It's not as if I landed up in the gutter, but there was a time ... the mental gutter, the emotional gutter is very uncomfortable ..."

To attempt to give this most upsetting part of Dusty's story a perspective, Pat Rhodes told me that the Dusty she knew in the late sixties went to live in California a quiet and really sweet person who rarely drank, never smoked and never swore. Pat and all Dusty's friends in Britain became very worried as they remarked, helplessly, on how she seemed to be falling further and further into a worse mire. It seemed she fell further each time she tried to pick herself up.

It gets worse. For Dusty to be able to have given this interview to Peter Evans, is, as I have said, a quantum psychological exorcism.

"Chemicals, you know, are always good for taking you outside yourself - INITIALLY. But finally they bring you down to earth with such a horrible crash that you can barely stand yourself at all. I very nearly went under with all that. Ironically, if you think about it at all, they were part and parcel of the trappings of success - having too much - not failure. Thank God I got out in time ... I never wanted to die. I wanted to go to sleep for a very long time, like Rip van Winkle. I wanted peace and I wanted quiet but I never wanted to do myself in. I suppose all those Catholic whatevers come at you when your mind begins to enter those murky waters. You go to hell, you know, if you kill

yourself ... Anyway, I discovered that I had a tremendous survival instinct. I'm a fighter at heart, I suppose ..."

The restrictive contractual arrangements she had forged with a management in whom she had so high initial hopes took two years to determine and it was 1977 before she decided to sign with a new manager, Barry Krost, himself lately arrived from London to make permanent residence in California. Dusty also had made contact with a prospective producer, Roy Thomas Baker, lately producer of the fast-rising British rock band QUEEN.

First, Barry.

I've never been one of the artists whom Barry has managed or agented over the years but I have been one of the many employees he has had. I was Barry's assistant for six years from 1970 until 1975. He had achieved prominence and power in the music industry through his management and association with Cat Stevens whose international career brought them both wealth and celebrity. But even Steve (Cat Stevens now called Yusuf Islam) had to contend with Barry's extended stable of artists. Barry also looked after Mike d'Abo, Colin Blunstone and Lewis Furey in the music stakes. He looked after Angela Lansbury and Peter Finch in the acting stakes as well as the careers of writers and film directors. He, with his partner Doug Chapin, was also hungry to break into film production which he was shortly to do with WHEN A STRANGER CALLS starring Barry's long time companion, the British actor Tony Beckley.

To the world at large, it must have also appeared that Barry Krost specialised in renaissance careers. Most of the aforementioned were on their second go around. Dusty? She must have seemed a tempting feather for Barry to put in his cap, maybe even likely to replace the gap left in Barry's stable by Cat Stevens' increasing withdrawal as he ventured further and further into the self-imposed monasticism of Islam.

Barry can make you feel like a million dollars when you decide to go with him. He also got people millions of dollars in highly lucrative deals. He made one with United Artists for Dusty and buoyed up by the confidence and zest and campy spirit of exuberance emanating from the compact little Barry, Dusty started to record. The resulting album was entitled IT

111

BEGINS AGAIN and that's what it must have felt like. Starting over.

Roy Thomas Baker was almost a perfect producer. Well used to the demands of another perfectionist, Freddie Mercury, his nature and character allowed him to slot immediately into the campy somewhat zany atmosphere which the interaction of Dusty Springfield and Barry Krost must have gathered around Dusty's career.

"Roy started his apprenticeship at Decca in the classical music division which immediately endeared him to me. Then he went through the Mantovani period and the Frank Chacksfields before becoming involved in contemporary pop and heavy rock. He has very broad musical tastes and so have I and that was necessary. There had to be an understanding, not necessarily a technical one where it had to be written down, but an appreciation of different kind of things ... of being aware of what sounds good whether it be Stravinsky or whatever. It worked out well with Roy from the start - we didn't even have any try-out sessions."

I'm sure Roy more than willingly acquiesced in the crediting of Dusty as 'Production Associate' on the label.

"... I had to do a lot of the leg work myself because Roy was involved in other projcts and I made a lot of decisions about the musicians. We went through all the material together and I decided which songs to do by watching the reaction on his face! He is the most under-stated person - if he says something is good or quite nice then it usually means it's terrific. It took me quite a while to read Roy - I had to talk to someone who had worked with him (Who?) and they explained that was how he was. I was crushed the first couple of times that I played him things and there was absolutely no reaction from him."

A generous spirit of revitalisation must have been abroad in the Golden State. All three on the 'team' were on a pilgrimage in a way, their grail being to either find or re-establish themselves. Being an entirely 'out' homosexual and so prominently successful at the time on the Hollywood Olympus, Dusty must have felt very comfortable with Barry Krost. She had never made any bones about how comfortable she felt in the company of her many gay friends and the selection of the songs on IT

BEGINS AGAIN reflected the instinct Barry and Roy Thomas must have had for the core of her audience for it was amongst the gays of the world that Dusty's memory had been kept most alive during her five previous wilderness years.

There had also been talk that she was to be produced by Gus Dudgeon, the producer of Elton John's first seminal albums. This was further compounded by rumours that Elton John had wanted her to record for his Rocket Records label with, so Dusty seems to have understood, Elton's hand on the fader knob.

"In retrospect, I'm rather glad I wasn't pulled into that - it wouldn't have worked because he wouldn't have had the time to spare. What counts in the studio is time and application though it might be different now with Elton because he isn't busy. (Oh yeah?) Then he was super-busy but I think that he did get quite carried away with the idea."

I have to say that at the time, Elton and John Reid still had Kiki Dee on their recording label. Our Kiki might not have been too thrilled ...

Anyway, I'D RATHER LEAVE WHILE I'M IN LOVE and LOVE ME BY NAME, a plaintive song about one night stands, are equally applicable to the straight as well as the gay element in Western society as it was developing post all the liberation movements of the activist seventies. SANDRA and HOLLYWOOD MOVIE GIRLS add to the poignancy, the latter also applying - with a quick change of gender - to the legions of handsome young men who also turn up daily in their droves and 'economy cars' at every Hollywood casting session. These are elemental songs, paeans to the dominant ethic of the dreams of America.

The IT BEGINS AGAIN songs were VERY carefully chosen. I think, of all her albums, they were Dusty's best-chosen repertoire. When the album and publicity photos appeared, there was Dusty, all cleaned up, looking great. And she sounded great. Somehow, Hollywood had again worked its magic influence but this time, directly, not via the anonymous, faraway silver screen. Dusty's chosen songs were part of a contemporary West Coast experience. Many of them had been written or co-written by women, at the forefront of a women's vanguard in music. Dusty had lived this life intimately and had experienced both the casualty rate as well as the 'perks' of success at first hand. of LOVE ME BY NAME she said to Keith Howes on GAY NEWS:

"I'd say I was into them (one night stands) mentally rather than physically. It was an attitude of whether anyone would accept the part of me that's Mary O'Brien rather than the person I'd created, Dusty Springfield. But if you set out to create a Dusty Springfield then you ask for problems."

I find Dusty very much at home with this material, analysing and communicating in song the fragile ecstasies and the hollow lows of life at the sharp end of the American dream. Dusty showed that she had learned from the experience of living by herself in a dream location that had gone sour on her.

"Actually, I'd never thought of LOVE ME BY NAME being that personal but it was written by Lesley Gore, a woman who became very successful as a singer very early on in her life - much as I did. She had a lot of record company executives flapping around her and she got totally lost. Now she has developed into a very nice human being. As for I'D RATHER LEAVE WHILE I'M IN LOVE, it doesn't relate to me at all. I'm hopeless at leaving before things get stale. I try to hang on with all my teeth to something that's gone down the drain. But, it's funny, that song sums up the professional side of me: I want to leave while it's still happening for me and not starting to slide back."

That she'd driven the freeways in her Pink Jensen Interceptor, that she'd loved a lot and dreamed her dreams of happiness only to have them shattered is not in question. That she USED this experience, like an actress interpreting a role, is obvious. Her vocal interpretations benefited on the most primal level from this ex-patriot life. She displays an artistic maturity, showing that she was clearly consummating her own artistic relationships, between herself and her material and between her art and her craft. The two were visible for the first time, in my opinion, seamlessly in tandem.

So, she DID make seamless in the end!

"DUSTY IN MEMPHIS is the only album of mine that I like although I didn't like it at the time it was released. I'm terribly

*predictable when it comes to my reactions of my own work.
IT BEGINS AGAIN is the first LP I have liked on first hearing - so
I hope that's not the kiss of death! My singing has changed - I
don't wince as much or yell and I don't try to overcome my vocal
limitations. I knew what they were before but I didn't pay any
attention. I was always singing songs I wasn't equipped to do
and the result was that two hours later my voice had gone ... I
want to get back into the studios and stockpile material so that
when I am doing concerts there won't be the pull which makes
me feel that I should really be working in the recording studios.
My last live appearances were at the London Palladium five
years ago although I have done some US shows since then. I
can't do the crazy pacings of the sixties now."*

So, it seemed that live performance career also beckoned.
It seemed she was ready to take Dusty Springfield out to the
people again. She did a show in Los Angeles at the Greek
Theatre as Peter Allen's special guest. From what she has said
very recently, it seems that her fears of being let down by
technical hitches and itchy technicians had been overcome by
the march of technology and progressive electronics.

*"It was wonderful the first time I came across a good
sound system. It was at The Greek. We borrowed Peter Allen's
and plus he used the Greek's sound which is very good because
you'd think the people at the back, being an amphitheatre, you'd
think it wouldn't reach but the sound really does reach the back.
There are a couple of dead spots round the side but he put extra
sound in. We shared it. It was the first time that I went, 'Oh, yes!
This is the way it's supposed to be. I'm having a great time' and
it was wonderful. It was, like, finally ... this is the way it's
supposed to be and I've been in a time warp all these years,
thinking that I know it's out there somewhere and actually
arriving in it from the Cannock Odeon and saying, 'This is the
way it SHOULD have been at the Cannock Odeon'."*

She sounds a happy girl. At one with herself and her art. I
wonder, if she could have renamed herself at this point in her
career, would she have done so and what would she have called
herself?

Could she have started again with Mary O'Brien?

"What's the worst thing (that could happen to me)? To

115

lose myself along the way just as I nearly lost myself before trying to hang on to that part of me that is Mary O'Brien as opposed to that part of me that is Dusty Springfield. And they ARE different. I still don't know who Mary O'Brien is but I know it's a decent human being. To lose sight of that would be the worst thing."

That she included I'M COMING HOME AGAIN on LIVING WITHOUT YOUR LOVE was, as so much of her song choices and titling had been before, almost prophetic. It was certainly almost too much for the audiences at the Drury Lane Theatre concerts she gave in London to promote IT BEGINS AGAIN and it's successor LIVING WITHOUT YOUR LOVE which had been produced by David Wolfert. I wasn't there but I'm assured that the audience were orgasmic in their rapture even at the merest hint of her possibly returning to London. Her work patently appeared heartfelt, from HER heart not from the disembodied pens of writers her audience couldn't see or hear. The lyrics of the songs had been made to reflect the life that had bred them, not merely pegged almost arbitrarily to a line of GUARDIAN in the person of Dave Gelly was at the Albert Hall Show.

"Glamourous she undoubtedly is but it is not the high camp glamour of Shirley Bassey. Her appeal is rather like that of a pantomime principal boy - good-natured, energetic and full of fun. She is the original un-soppy girl, a kind of rock 'n' roll Joan Hunter Dunn ... She is still in charge of her personality and free to employ it to devastating effect on stage."

It was twenty years since she'd become a Lana Sister. It's a long way from SEVEN LITTLE GIRLS to SANDRA.

Chapter Fourteen

Wherever I hang my hat ...

So what went wrong? Why did the reality appear to buckle under its own weight? The vaunted management relationships shattered and so, perhaps concomitantly, did the relationships with United Artists. Dusty kind of de-mobilised herself yet again. It must be very hard to have had to be everything else to yourself in your life except yourself ...

Three years went by before she recorded again. The world changed and the rattling music business snake sloughed another skin. But the ever-lengthening snake slithered past Dusty. It must have been awful, feeling that you weren't even tempting enough to be considered prey.

"... things became so global. If you went that far (to America) you were assumed not to be working and vice versa. If you were here (Britain) America didn't know about you. It's only gradually that it's become so global, music in general. It's not so insular. It's still CAPABLE of being insular but the last ten years have been an awful lot of leaps and bounds - satellites and things. So you can't wear the same dress any more. It used to be great, you could hop from country to country and wear the same dress. You can't anymore because if you do BBC 1, it's shown in Holland and probably part of Germany and you never know which part of Germany so that's that dress out of the window."

Dusty's career has always seemed to be to be analogous to a river running through a very populous land, naturally finding its own level and generally flowing to rejoin other water. Mostly, both its course and potential have been taken for granted and the River Dusty has therefore merely meandered, meeting an obstacle only to meekly flow round it. The river has never been damned, it has never been held back in order to wash the obstacle away in a torrent of strength. No canals have ever been cut for it to flow more profitably for its own sake. No real use has ever been made of the innate force inherent in the very water itself. Such diversions and alternative courses that were available were never occupied.

"But two acting coaches of great stature saw me sing at a benefit and they've offered to give me lessons ... Nice to explore ... I don't know whether it will lead anywhere ... I think acting would help round myself out in some ways ..."

Mary O'Brien had been to drama classes, years and years before in Ealing. It didn't last then. Instead, Mary had created Dusty Springfield. Control. Control. Dusty Springfield's is definitely a female career. It is the way I have observed many women behaving in their relationships with either men or women and in their marriages. It is a way that a single female will walk through a roomful of men. A single man, on the other hand, would never walk through a roomful of women. And, although more obviously female, this passive behaviour which I'm attempting to describe ultimately has nothing to do with gender but everything to do with role. It has to do with power. And survival. Sheer existence.

The songs on IT BEGINS AGAIN and LIVING WITHOUT YOUR LOVE had a sense of the victim about them. Songs with that basic 'hard done by' but 'still struggling on' appeal have always done well. They mean a great deal to everyone who feels that they are suffering or have suffered and have been unable to voice and therefore exorcise their pain. These songs seemed to bleed real blood. Of course the penitent and the faithful want their virgins to cry real tears and to bleed real blood. Doing so is THEIR salvation; the same, almost cannibalistic, relationship that exists between the fans and their divae.

Do we remember Dusty saying twenty years before that

she's not the legendary type? That she would never go through the necessary suffering? Slash the wrists? Dusty Springfield's wandering years may have decreased her stature in the eyes of Mary and Dusty but they increased it many times and manifold in the hearts and minds of the faithful fans. If art really does imitate life, then the art and the artist inevitably become inextricably linked in the eyes and ears of the punters. The punter is paying, essentially, for a slice of life.

Graham Lock, writing in New Musical Express in 1978, appraised most accurately: *"She's working in the dark - no other woman singer has followed a similar career so there's no example to follow."* Dusty was still writing her own rules but it's tough being in control when there's nothing to control.

The theme for these further years of enforced idleness she'd already sung. *"Mama said there'd be days like this, there'd be days like this my mama said ..."* Trouble is, I don't think days like these had EVER been envisaged, at least, not in terms of years of them. Precisely WHAT Dusty had envisaged for her forties and thereafter I know not. I just know it wasn't this. Nothing was going particularly well. Not even love. It seems that now Dusty was being almost forced into living being the victim instead of merely acting it out.

"They were circumstances I should never have been in but that women get themselves into. I've been in that trap that I've seen other women in, you get so frightened that you are ashamed to tell anyone what's going on. You retreat. I did get myself out in the end - it had been a very destructive relationship."

In 1982 she recorded WHITE HEAT for Casablanca.

"Every time I make an album, the company I'd made it for would get swallowed up. They'd fire everyone you'd been working with and the enthusiasm would disappear with them. Twentieth century Fox was the original company which got swallowed up by a re-activated Casablanca which then got eaten up by Phonogram. Then I had to fire the original producer (André Fisher) because he had put half the budget up his nose ... there was a point where I began to feel that I was just some company's tax loss."

Dusty said the same thing to HELLO! Magazine as the snake went for companies instead of artists:

119

"Two companies I was with were swallowed up by larger ones. Amidst all the corporate shuffle I was left on the shelf."

WHITE HEAT was released in America in 1982, never in Britain where it was only available as an import. But Dusty was accredited producer together with Howard Steele, the engineer who replaced the sacked André Fisher. Andy d'Addario is credited as engineer. Again, Dusty maintained the seeming reality of the symbiosis between her life and her art. The songs were once again superbly chosen if symbiosis was indeed the bill they were intended to fit.

On SOFT CORE she sings, 'I'm sick of being submissive when I feel like I want to scream.' SOFT CORE went down a storm with her hard core audience. She had songs written for her by Elvis Costello - LOSING YOU - and by Sting who wrote the lyrics, 'We could be lovers but I don't think we can ever be friends'. Very eighties.

All the reviews seem to remark on the sureness of what they perceived as a new direction, of how contemporary and relevant her work had always been and so remained. Graham Lock wrote in NME: *"WHITE HEAT roars with a relentless energy that galvanises Dusty into her most confident and COMMITTED singing for years. That's a real bonus because Dusty Springfield is about the best pop singer Britain ever produced ... SOFT CORE is a different kettle of fissure - a stark ballad of sexual ambivalence on which her voice superbly underscores a queasy feeling that's equal parts desire and despair ... I can't think of anyone I'd rather welcome back to pop stardom and after WHITE HEAT I can't think of anyone likely to come back with such style and power and grace."*

Way to go, Graham!

Irony saw to it that Dusty was returned to Phonogram after the brief deviation that corporate shenanigans took her from the true the tried and the tested. So why, with reviews like that, did Phonogram never issue WHITE HEAT? Ever? Why not do it now?

1983 and 1984, publicly, saw very little happening to La Dust except her widely reported going to work for a Los Angeles animal sanctuary.

"People think it's cute to have a lion cub but it grows up

into a lion. They think it's elegant but then it starts chewing up the sofa and jumping at you from the tops of doorways ... It's tough being a singer but if a three hundred pound bear jumps on you, it's tougher. Also, shovelling shit proved to be a very levelling experience."

But unbeknownst to Dusty, her reputation in her homeland had been growing in younger, curious and appreciative minds. Whilst Dusty'd been away in America, pop music in Britain had come of age. Yesterday's news became current headlines as a whole new generation of intelligent young people sought credence for the state of the music they loved in the works of pop's past. Dusty's legend hadn't tarnished at all. It was alive and well and, became, to her obvious delight, a cult as she found herself metamorphosed yet again from past pop singer to prototype pop diva. What the kids ask for on the dance floor gets noticed not only by the DJ's but obviously by the nightclub bosses.

Step forward Peter Stringfellow.

Peter owned nightclubs. STRINGFELLOW'S, THE HIPPO-DROME, the latest incarnation of the pleasuredrome that once was an old stamping ground of Dusty's, THE TALK OF THE TOWN.

Peter's and Dusty's may have been a euphoric courtship but their's was a disastrous marriage. They were inspired opposites. He was a businessman who played records; she was a diva/producer who made them. Lately, too, she'd been making albums. She'd been doing it rather well. This fabulous foray into club-land was, surely, all about singles or was Peter Stringfellow so innocent of the ways of the record business and, indeed, of recording artists that he actually thought he could start a record company by merely writing a cheque? And Dusty ... NEVER invite the backer into the rehearsals and keep the money box and the control box as far apart as possible. This is basic A, B, C of The Biz, isn't it?

"Peter knew fuck all about the record industry. And to make it worse he wouldn't listen to my advice. My relationship with him was one of the incidents that made me so fed up with the business. I nearly gave up for good ..."

To Adam Sweeting in THE GUARDIAN, she expands:

"... I didn't know Peter had a fetish for butterflies. He has

them everywhere. I present him with a song called SOMETIMES LIKE BUTTERFLIES and he goes, 'Yes! We'll put it out in an eight minute version and it will be number one!' I say, 'I don't think so ...' Peter is the most marvellous club person and I really respect what he's done but he wasn't a record person. It didn't work. He still sends me flowers every now and again but he's just such a mixture of being abusive publicly to me and being a gentleman."

So, maybe the work, SOMETIMES LIKE BUTTERFLIES and I WANNA TAKE CONTROL wasn't of the very best but, seen for it's best, the venture restored Dusty to the public eye and particularly to the field of vision of Neil Tennant and Chris Lowe, collectively THE PET SHOP BOYS who were enjoying a success which in post-Modern pop terms they seem to continuously re-invent.

The 'phone bell rang one day in America. Seems they wanted to re-invent Dusty Springfield.

" ... Yes. That was a watershed in my life, really and it was just meant to happen. It just sort of plopped into my life and changed it. I'd gone through a very down time. Nothing was happening. I wasn't well and ... I was gradually pulling myself together. I was sitting in someone's garden in California under one of the few trees that were there and a feeling came over me that it was all going to be all right, everything was going to be all right. I don't know where the feeling came from. What came back into me was either the innate conceit or the stupidity of the first time around, starting up without any connections, without any knowledge, with being as naive as I was. I just knew that everything was going to be all right. I knew that I was going to have hits. I just knew it. But I didn't know how. I just knew it was going to happen and that happened to me under that tree and it was either the same afternoon or the next day that I got a 'phone call from Vicki about the song (WHAT DID I DO TO DESERVE THIS?) Somebody sent a tape to me. I got this 'phone call and I knew who they (THE PET SHOP BOYS) were because I nearly had an accident on the freeway listening to WEST END GIRLS and I thought, 'Who's that? What is that? Who are they, I've got to know?' and gradually I got tuned into them.

Because they started to get really big there ... I knew it wasn't American but I didn't know who THE PET SHOP BOYS were ... They've always had a ... Well, there's a symphonic quality to it, a larger than life quality to it. Fullness and ... I don't know ... They struck me in that way, that kind of off-handedness, not really trying very hard ... There's a lot going on but essentially, then ... It was almost spoken against quite a lot going on. It's hard to pick out what was going on but it was full. There was a pulse to it and I just loved that sound. No one had done that sound. So, I suppose, it struck me the first time I heard Phil Spector ... 'Funny how potent cheap music can be'. Never in a million years thought about working with them ..."

There was someone she'd been more than thinking of working with and that person was Richard Carpenter, solo since Karen's premature and untimely death.

"It was actually Richard who looked me up first. I'd just done an AOR (Adult Oriented Rock) record with him when I was contacted by Neil and Chris."

Vicki Wickam had a great deal to do with this introduction. She engendered it and then fostered it, feeling her way and choosing her moments as do all good managers with fragile clients.

"I used to get really fed up with her," Vicki told Robin Katz on MUSIC WEEK in 1990, *"complaining about her career, her management and whatever else. Plus I wanted to kick her in the behind because she sat vegetating in Los Angeles for so long. I'm a vocal freak and to me, Dusty Springfield is one of the top five vocalists in the world and singers like her shouldn't get lost."*

The tape which Vicki had duly arranged to be sent to California arrived and found a welcome amongst all 'the feelings' Dusty had been having.

"Vicki said, I think, something like, 'They need to know fairly fast. Would you work with them?' Not knowing which part of the song they wanted me to do or anything and I think it must have been five minutes later ... I said, 'Yes' and it was a carry-on of 'the feeling'. I came to London to do it with them, still not knowing what they wanted me to do. But then I never knew what they wanted me to do and they didn't really know until we sort of worked it out and I remember going in the studio and really

mucking the song up because it didn't occur to me that Neil was too polite to tell me. They were being very polite and very quiet and I said, 'What is it you want?' and they said, 'The sound of your voice'. I said, 'You mean, just sing it?' and they said, 'Yes'".

And that was when my life began to get simpler. I just didn't realise that that's what they wanted. I thought they wanted much more from me, much more decorative, much more wild, much more involved. Basically, they just wanted me to sing ... 'Since you went away, I've been hanging around ...' That's what they wanted and they were right."

But Dusty was being very, very cautious. She hadn't come to stay ... Only to see.

But it had brought her finally together with Vicki Wickham who took over her management. Vicki had long been domiciled in New York where she had been managing LABELLE and then individually the singer/writer Nona Hendryx. With Vicki as her manager as well as, obviously, still being her closest friend, it seems that some kind of career course had been re-plotted.

The duet WHAT HAVE I DONE TO DESERVE THIS? gave Dusty yet another extension to the ladder of her life.

"... I've liked it (the electro/techno/disco sound of THE PET SHOP BOYS) for a long time because it was all the sounds I wanted to make in the sixties. I was quietly listening to them and enjoying them, much more of the European stuff which we sometimes got in California ... we get it a lot now but at that time it was quite new and I was so delighted to hear my musical dreams coming true that I just rushed at the idea, that it would be wonderful to be enveloped in that and consistently I've been very happy since I've been working with THE PET SHOP BOYS, to be rapped in that because it's what I've always wanted. It's heaven for me. Musically I'm having a heck of a good time."

In 1989 a solo single NOTHING HAS BEEN PROVED was recorded for the film SCANDAL.

"That was such an incredible song. I mean, it really was a gem and you know, the fact that it was a hit I know had a lot to do with them. The fact they had written it. But there again, there's a lyric that, to half it's audience, nobody understood a word of but it didn't matter because it had a sound ... Originally

they had written it (IN PRIVATE) for SCANDAL because it would have tied in very well - the words, 'What you gonna say?' and 'What you gonna do in public?' The idea had obviously been pushed around a bit. They weren't sure what the music was going to be, the film people. I suppose this was at the very beginning of the idea for the film. Maybe they'd approached THE PET SHOP BOYS or something. Maybe Palace Pictures had approached them, I don't know but I do know that song originally started, not finished, with the thought of being in the film. Subsequently the film chose to use original stuff from the sixties - early sixties, late fifties. But IN PRIVATE had real value, quite separate from the film ...It's just a straight ahead, anyone can sing it song. It works in pubs ... I thought it was a really good pop song, really good pop song. Great."

I've often wondered why Sandie Shaw didn't sing on this movie. Her husband, Nick, was one of the directors of Palace. If Sandie HAD been asked, wasn't Dusty thrilled to have been second choice? Sandie was, after all, pretty much involved with her own comeback with Morrissey. This just left Lulu, really and she would have her turn in the years to come with TAKE THAT. Quite a series of blind dates ... and there we have Cilla. Nothing sets off an old broad as much as a good honest toy boy.

"I'm really grateful to THE PET SHOP BOYS and I feel embarrassed to say that. It sticks in my craw to BE grateful. I am, because THEY had the faith in me that I didn't have. They saw something in me that I was about to lose."

Inevitable comparisons were raised with other songwriting teams with whom she'd been closely associated. In RECORD MIRROR in 1990, Dusty acknowledged the passage of at least a generation, from Bacharach and David to Tennant and Lowe:

"They seem as if they're very special people with a special talent. Burt Bacharch was a major force in pop music. He was classically trained and used techniques and arrangements that had never been used in pop music ... When THE PET SHOP BOYS came out, they were very different too - I can't remember anyone singing like Neil does before. They're innovators."

THE PET SHOP BOYS singles heralded a co-operation which produced the album REPUTATION released in 1990.

"God knows (what would have happened if THE PET

SHOP BOYS hadn't come along) I just would have taken a different route. It would have probably been more scenic. I was plotting a bit over in California, wondering how I was going to approach all this again and then all the decisions were taken out of my hands which I was very relieved about. It's always with hindsight that I realise things blindingly clearly but WHAT HAVE I DONE TO DESERVE THIS? was a great rehearsal for the next one NOTHING HAS BEEN PROVED. It's as if I'm being weaned in some way and allowed to rehearse things little by little."

Had Dusty's 'simpler' life resulted in an easier ride in the studios? Had she, in becoming the diva, been able to relieve some of the neurotic pressure? Let go a bit ... Just sing? It wasn't something she was used to. REPUTATION was produced by seven people in all, Neil Tennant and Chris Lowe, Dusty, Brian Spence, Dan Hartman and Rupert Hine with Andy Richard credited for REPUTATION the single. Such a little pie for so many fingers.

"I want to work with them again but I'm sure neither side ALWAYS wants to work together. With the album being a mixture, I'm being given things to do that gradually build up the confidence and allow me a little more freedom ... The record is fairly eclectic in tempos. I would be somewhat distraught to have to go and make a dance record with somebody more frivolous than THE PET SHOP BOYS because it really wouldn't work. With them, there's always something slightly off centre that I like. I'm a bit off-centre as well. We get along fine."

So WHY didn't THE PET SHOP BOYS produce all of it? Could it all be to do with that painful formula of knowing what you don't want not being the same as knowing what you want?

REPUTATION was issued to mixed reviews. Reviews are never critical appreciation. They're about something else; a subjective perception in the reviewer controls the audio/visual experience so that yesterdays's dinner, last night's glass too much, this mornings domestic tiff, an innate dislike of nostalgia, an inherent aversion to sentimentality ... Whatever.

But when people complain about bad reviews, do they remember ever to question the good ones? Is the praise as ill-deserved sometimes as the admonishment. I think they're the same people who complain that God hasn't answered their prayer. My guess is that the prayer has been answered: God's merely said 'No'.

But there were many people who saw the sense, who positively assessed Dusty's work.

"... songs that cunningly explore the pitfalls of fame and the way they're mirrored in private lives," Adam Sweeting wrote in THE GUARDIAN.

And I, for another, think they were great songs. Dusty was still managing to choose some crackers although from what she says, it seems that some divine hand plays its part in guiding her facility.

"Strangely enough, I very seldom listen to lyrics but that (REPUTATION) was so sort of campy and relevant that I couldn't resist it. Although the original song was actually quite different from what it is now. We had to make quite a lot of changes because it was more like a rock song and it's a credit to Andy Richard's that he took it away from that."

At what point, I wonder does she judge the point worthy of abandoning a great tune because she finds the lyrics don't match up? It can be an expensive business.

"I wanted them (Neil and Chris) to produce the whole LP but I think they wanted it to be just half them. I don't want to fall out with them. It's ended up sounding like two different albums."

That there were no concerts, no dates, no live performances must have been greatly to Dusty's relief. Video had come to the rescue.

"WHAT HAVE I DONE TO DESERVE THIS? was my first video and I had no idea what to do and they had no idea that I had no idea what to do and I had to keep asking somebody. I hadn't got a clue what you were supposed to do on videos. I didn't know about looking cameras and stuff like that. With all my television stuff, I never bothered about cameras. I just sort of went floundering around and if they followed me fast enough that was all right. It never occurred to me that shots were worked out."

She soon learned. When video-time came around for NOTHING HAS BEEN PROVED,

" ... I looked very strange. I was not, er ... I didn't like the

way I looked in that but you know in hindsight, I see actually it's very well done. I didn't really know what they were doing but by then, you know, I sort of knew what the cameras were doing, you know - not a clue on the other one."

Dusty's association with THE PET SHOP BOYS, however it was going to pan out in the future, decided one thing for her and that was that her life in California had been lived. The initial desire to leave somewhere she felt threatened and spied upon and to settle where she could be anonymous and yet public had been fulfilled. It was a state she had never been able to achieve whilst living in Britain. Years into the move to California, the original longing for the lotus-eating life had obviously either been slaked or proved unworkable. Ten years after she sang about it, Dusty found herself coming home again although this involved an eighteen month bridging residence near Amsterdam, supposedly because it was the nearest place to London to which she could relocate her cats without having to be forcibly parted from them in a quarantined cattery in Great Britain.

Dusty and her cats. A pretty fabled union.

"I think they're amazingly beautiful and sensuous. They get up in the morning and they look great. They're comic and affectionate and they can see a phoney straightaway."

I think that begs the question ... Yes. That remark could almost be how Mary and Dusty see Dusty Springfield. Tragically, having come such a very long and circuitous route from California and having been so patient and waiting so long, one of the two cats Dusty had at the time of the release of REPUTATION was killed. She must have been heartbroken.

"... she got run over but the other one definitely is in England's green and pleasant land. There's just one now. I'll get some more but it's not fair at the moment. I'm not there much ... in fact, I think I'll go home after this and clean out the cat box. If ever you think you're getting a big head or you're getting tired ... that levels you out."

To Chrissy Iley, recounting the same experience, she expanded on the one that survived:

"The other one, Nicholas Nicholaievich is fine but he hates me. It's so sad, because I like him." Dusty goes on to answer Chrissie's question as to whether Dusty thinks she likes Nicholas

more because he doesn't like her. *"Yes, it makes me struggle with him more."*

Love me, dammit. Love me!

And as Chrissie Iley points out, this would seem a terribly masochistic relationship which she fears may be a metaphor for Dusty's life. Dusty just wants to be loved, by man, woman or cat.

The Dusty who returned to the round of interviews, press conferences, photo calls was by turns reflective and philosophical and ultra-sensitive to the demands celebrity in 1990's Britain made. She told the interviewer on the REPUTATION video when he enquired about making mistakes:

"Oh, it's quite easy to make them again ... It (the machine taking you over) usually does and sometimes I feel that now but it's ... experience is something you don't even realise you've got until you're in a situation where you have to use it and without even realising that it's there it helps you to deal with something and it keeps you more level. I'm glad I had all that. I'm glad I'm not doing it for the first time. I seem so far able to handle it a bit better. We'll see."

Chrissey Iley elicited a very balanced interview. Two different quoted versions of the same source material appear in CASHBOX and the DAILY MAIL in 1990. The MAIL quoted Dusty thus:

"... I do care (about what people whisper) ... I go through very vulnerable stages. But once you realise you're vulnerable, it can make you tough and deal with things better. I thought I was shatter-proof but I'm actually made of very thin glass. I know I don't have to stay (in Britain) that it's all right to say, 'It hurts'. If it turns out sour for me here, I'll leave. I don't know why I put up with California for so long. I suppose because I've always been besotted with doing the American dream. It was bad but I put up with it. But I won't anymore. The same with a relationship. I used to think I had to put up with the pain. Not any more. I care terribly about me again."

Not to easy to be able to do in private. Being interviewed in 1987 for WHAT HAVE I DONE TO DESERVE THIS?, Dusty is emphatic concerning her feelings about being recognised.

"... but in a shop, oh, that's the worst. Or in a cafe on the M1 with people staring. Or in a supermarket. I can't wait to get

out. I feel uncomfortable because I can't be me ... I've got to be Dusty Springfield." The girl who invented Dusty Springfield, as she admitted herself, in order to GET noticed, must have been having some tardy second thoughts and some impracticable regrets.

It seemed that Dusty's life and career had left too many un-turned stones for the press and media juggernaut to give her prodigal homecoming anything less than a bumpy ride.

" ... for some reason, I'm finding it (being hounded by tabloid journalists) rather difficult to handle. I went through so much before at that level that I was sort of naive enough to think that nobody would want to do it again and they do. I actually find it quite upsetting. I'm not flattered by it at all because some very nasty things have happened in terms of other people being abused by that ... and people get killed that way. However, I'm trying not to get paranoid about it."

She must have found being under the spotlight once again unbearable.

"All of a sudden, they're out (side her house) there with telephoto lenses. I thought they must be really hard up for news. Why do they want to take a picture of me taking my rubbish out? I have absolutely nothing to hide. I live with my cat. That's it. That's my life ... It backfires if you talk to them and it backfires if you don't ... I chose this job. Nobody forced it down my throat. So either you stand it or you get out."

Still that old problem of the public Dusty Springfield and the private Dusty. It seemed that from remarks made on the REPUTATION video, thirty five years of the public/private problem of her split-level existence had furnished few answers.

"... I'm sort of almost schizophrenic about having a private life and I don't like things to suddenly interfere with that 'cos it's my only peace and quiet and I get very much into being quiet and sort of just running around with my cat and that I find it very intrusive. I mean, I over-react to an intrusion into that but once I put on my show persona ... a show, then I'm perfectly happy doing that. I'm not good at mixing the two. Some people are much better at that sort of blurring the edges but I do like two separate lives and sometimes it doesn't work out that way."

At first, life seemed as though it could be sweet again in 1990 in England's pleasant pastures green.

"I could cry at a field of corn. Sometimes I think I'm not adapting to England. Then I'll go for a drive and come across some particular stretch of river and it makes me cry because it's so beautiful. I can't go to films because I cry at everything and my mascara runs ... I can't deal with abrasive people, it makes me jittery and when I get home I'm shaking ... I think I've been very lucky. There have been a few real bum people in my life. But basically I attract nice people ... I have fits of abysmal stupidity. Confessional mode. Bah! It's to do with my Catholic upbringing ..."

I'm sure in Los Angeles, Dusty also had neighbours. It's just that nobody talks to their neighbours there. Borrowing cups of sugar and neighbourhood watch is something that maids and armed response companies take care of. But, down Buckinghamshire way, people tend to be friendlier, I find.

"Do you know, it's the first time I've ever had neighbours. They're really nice. One was a customs officer who caught lots of drug runners, one owns a rubber factory, one runs a security systems company and one's a schoolteacher in a posh school. They're not the least bit impressed by what i do for a living. We do normal neighbourly things like have barbecues. Everyone just sits on the stairs and laughs. It's a whole new experience for me ... They're not at all entranced by me. They like me because ... I'm actually quite a nice person."

But, although she was back, was Dusty here to stay? After the razzmatazz of another album launch, without work, not being a songwriter, with no current commitment for further product, no live performances, no tour or live dates, life can get very lonely in the Buckinghamshire countryside for a woman in her early fifties professing only a cat for company, neighbours or no ... Three years on in 1993, Dusty mused, achingly reflective:

"I feel trapped if I'm anywhere for more than a year. Although, as you get older, it becomes harder to be a gypsy ... It definitely runs in the family. My brother and I are incapable of sitting still in one place for more than three months without being absolutely crushingly bored. But it does get harder - when

you have responsibilities and mortgages and all of that stuff. I should never ever buy a house because I realise now what a trap it is. It is sort of a good idea at the time - it's what people do. It shows you're grown up. It shows you're mature. But, actually, I didn't know what a mortgage was and I went into shock when I discovered that I actually owned about three bricks of the house. I think I'd rather just pay rent - because at least there's a lease and you can get out of it ... It's just, I'm a transient ... I have always wanted to be somewhere else - which I learnt isn't always the best idea - because the old grass is always greener ... I know it's not, but it's just a restlessness in me and my neighbours find it very sad. They say, 'Poor Mary. I don't find it sad at all but I was beginning them that it was sad until - I have these late night talks with my brother. We never see each other but we have these late night talks and he said, 'Don't lose that'. And he put me straight. He said, 'That's what keeps you interested and if you don't have that you'd vegetate'. And it's true. I don't find it sad at all. There are times when it FEELS sad. There are times when I sit on the steps at the back or I walk around the garden and I think, 'What am I DOING here' and I watch the planes go over because I don't live too far from the airport. And I used to go, when I got really nuts with that feeling. I'd just drive to the airport so I could watch the planes closer, which is odd because I really don't like planes particularly. I love airports - I love watching people at airports. I got very morose about a year and a half ago. Nothing was happening. Just nothing was happening with my career and my personal life. Anything. So I just used to drive to the airport and watch other people. Well, there are such dramas that go on at airports. It's all very moving. It's people saying goodbye or it's people weeping goodbye or it's people greeting and I love it 'cause you can sit there late at night and you can just eat crap and be totally impersonal (anonymous?). Nobody cares 'cause they're all busy doing whatever they're doing, going somewhere ... But I love watching what's going on. I hate airports when I'm travelling ... I don't like them when I'm actually having to travel."

In you keep travelling, keep on the move, when you throw a memory out of the window, like litter, you don't ever have to bother much with where it comes to be finally buried. Some-body else has to bother with that.

Peter Evans quoted a very close friend of Dusty's in an article he wrote fifteen years ago:

"Dear Dusty, she could always feel a dead sea beneath her particular crest of a wave."

Dusty remembers back to her childhood:

"My parents ... they really hated being there (High Wycombe) ... I mean, it was the end of the world for them to be that far from London so they never unpacked ... My father never cut the grass- the neighbours' chickens used to go in there - Honest to God - we never saw them again. It was great for kids because it was like a hunting ground for all sorts of things. But they kept saying, 'Oh, we're going back to London and I still do that myself. I'm transient. They brought both their children up to be very transient ... As my brother says, 'There's another motel down the road'. There's a title of a book, somewhere. Nothing would please me more than to just leave the door open and put the cat in my arms and go."

CHAPTER FIFTEEN

We only have one life to live.
But she has two, already lived...

In 1990, Dusty said to Laura Lee Davies:

"What I'm singing right now is fine but it'd be nice to do an album of really good old standards if there's anything left of me after all this. I wasn't raised on this kind of music."

She was referring to the material she'd recorded on REPUTATION. So what next?

"Maybe country," she continued, "they really appreciate someone with a few sad songs to sing and a story to tell ... they really like sequins too!"

As I write, Dusty Springfield is recording again in Nashville. In America. Where she got away from.

Vicki Wickham explained on BBC Radio 2 documentary. Charting the main course of Dusty's progress through three and half professional decades:

"She's just signed to Sony Records in the UK and a worldwide deal. Lovely managing director called Kit Crones ... Was a real fan and wanted to work with her and she's going to Nashville in January (1994) and is going to do a sort of - it's not a country album, not DUSTY SINGS COUNTRY but it's very much Dusty with great songs which she's already - she and the producer - have selected quite a few, but with a country feel to it. A country flavour which after all isn't that far from R and B and going back to THE SPRINGFIELDS ... It's where they started

with folk and country so ... That's what the next record's going to be."

Was the Springfield wheel coming full circle?

Dusty, speaking in November '93, complemented her manager's perception of the work ahead:

"Yeah, so much is going to happen - All or nothing. It's hard to talk about something you haven't experienced. There's going to be a lot of experience, good or bad or indifferent but it will have happened and it will be fresh. To me, it's much easier to talk about something that's just happened to you ... I'm trying to keep an open mind. I do know that somewhere along the line I had an idea, it was two years ago, that I wanted to do an album, not country and western music or be a country singer because I can't, but something that had a country slant to it or used influences from country music and to take advantage of the writers that were there. I always remember being there (with THE SPRINGFIELDS) and it seemed the walls were alive with writers coming out of them and some were good and some were bad. But the volume! And also being there, the ... And this was just with THE SPRINGFIELDS and I was told it hadn't changed on that level ... That once the buzz starts, incredible numbers of songs come through. I'm never going to be the type that leaps up and down about the idea of going into a recording studio. It's not my favourite place to be. It's an un-natural thing to do. If someone said to me, 'You've got to record another album in Shepherds Bush,' I would probably hit them. Now, if someone said to me, 'You can record the album at Checkenden Outside Studios', which is down near Wallingford in Oxfordshire (Berkshire?), I wouldn't hit them at all, I'd hug them. It's that it seems to be my destiny to record in Shepherds Bush so ... There you try to get away from the studio. You walk outside and it's louder outside than it is inside and I just thought, 'Well, I'm not going to get, probably, to record in these manor houses in the country ...' Because my career doesn't seem to ... People don't seem to want to do that with me so let's go to Nashville and see how it works and I really have an open mind and once again I have this uncanny feeling that it's going to be all right. That either makes me optimistic or stupid, I'm not sure which."

Poor Shepherds Bush.

Dusty is certainly not stupid. She always has grounds for optimism. As long as she can sing, she will always have her 'feeling' that things will be all right.

"I've made friends with my limitations, they're no longer the enemy I have to battle against. Knowing what I can and can't do gives me so much more freedom."

For a quixotic lady who has tilted at many windmills, it seems that there is still wind enough to turn the sails again. This time it is the record giant Sony - father and mother to George Michael and Michael Jackson - that is putting its money where its mouthpiece is, prepared to invest hundreds and thousands of dollars into making Dusty Springfield a star yet again ... Not only because of her name and certainly not on the track record which is patchy to say the least but because of that which I have deliberately left until last.

The voice.

If her voice was a flower, there would be a Latin name for it. It would be classified as VOX SPRINGFIELDIAE or VOX DUSTIA.

It was not until quite late that she became or was made aware that her voice was anything remarkable.

"Probably not 'til fourteen or something like that. Because while I knew I could do things that were different and that made me a bit of an oddball, I'd no idea that one could actually USE them. Because, remember, I'd ... And I think, probably, it was only after I started listening to Peggy Lee and people like that, Ella Fitzgerald, that I thought maybe I could use this voice somehow. But I wasn't, I don't think I was even calculating how to use it. I just knew that I didn't want to be a librarian but I didn't know how NOT to be a librarian ..."

There is in existence a recording of an Italian medley which Dusty made when she was very young; she mentions eleven years of age although I've heard thirteen.

"I've got them somewhere at home and they're real collectors' items ... It's the equivalent of a home movie but sound wise. You actually can ... we sound pretty much the same, which was really odd - to have that voice. People talk about talent and this and that and the other - no! One has a gift or one doesn't have a gift. A gift is a gift - what you make of it is the talent, I

think. Just staying on your feet is the talent. Above all you need to be strong and healthy. That's really more what you need than anything. It's great, it has a real atmosphere and it just kind of says it all in as far as how, how much it's true that people are given gifts in life because, as rough as it is, it's quite obvious who it is (singing) and, at that age, where did that come from? I mean, neighbours didn't sound like that, nobody I knew sounded like that. It had a lot to do with my parents and my brother - to do with influence. I probably wouldn't have sung at all if it wasn't been for the musical influences I had. So they were gifts too."

She maintains that in the early solo years she over-used the famous pipes, shouted too hard and strained for notes that were too high, being under the impression that that's what was expected of her.

"The craziest times were nineteen sixty four, sixty five, they were murderous. You had to have a lot of stamina. It was a lot of fun too but the physical drudgery gets to you in the end."

Laryngitis and tonsilitis started to become constant threats. The physical strain of her schedule as well as her tautly strung emotional bow both contributed to her constant anticipation of throat or larynx infections.

"In Australia and New Zealand, they worked us until we were really worn out. We'd have either twelve hours on a train or three or four 'plane changes every day. And some of the halls in which we played were very grim. It got to such a pitch that we just had to put our foot down."

Dusty went to Martin Laurence, the American voice coach, who helped her understand her totally untrained instrument. From Laurence she got exercise tapes which she still uses to warm up the precious pipes.

"I have very little technical expertise. Training really is breathing and using your vocal equipment properly. I'm afraid that I just don't do it. I mean well when I go on-stage but I lose contact with any form of discipline. I've always gone for that end effect and to hell with the cost. I really want to please the people and I'll do it any way I can."

But she is ever critical, not only critical but self-deprecating, ruthlessly so to the point of masochism, to the point where you cannot believe that SHE doesn't believe she has done something superb with her priceless, unique voice.

"... I lose sight of its value, I really do. I've never quite got that ... got it. There have been a few times when I've really liked something I've done and then I see its value and the only time I see its value is in defiance. But then that's me. That's been my life in that, 'Don't tell me I can't do that', or, 'I can do that better'. But if someone says, 'We want you to do such and such,' I will always go, 'Why?' Because at that point in the asking or on the occasion I don't understand the value of the sound of my voice. And then I will hear something that I've done that gives me chills. It's usually years afterwards and then I'll go, 'THAT'S what they meant!' But I never get it at the time."

Well, I get it. My Nigel gets it. My friend David got it, gets it and hopefully will go on getting it. Our nieces, one generation removed, get it and they got it with no prompting from us. Me and him and them and the Dusty Springfield Fan Club members and the record company executives and the songwriters and the producers and the engineers and the musicians and the gophers and the journalists and the countless thousands and hundreds and thousands who have gone out and parted with their hard-earned - they all got it!

I can't have been the only lonely teenager shut up in a boarding school who can still, thirty years later, weep on cue when I hear the intro to I JUST DON'T KNOW WHAT TO DO WITH MYSELF. I still remember that aching pit of loneliness I scrabbled in and the desperation to have anyone just to hug me. Dusty's songs made all that painful adolescence seem bearable, 'cos there was someone else who knew what I was going through. Her gender and the fact she was singing about 'him' and 'my man' made absolute sense to me with my ridiculous crushes on unrequitable heroes ... I'm sure a whole generation of gay boys as well as straight boys and straight girls and gay girls and Uncle Tom Cobleys and all grew up with Dusty Springfield as their very best and often only friend. I danced with her - she was THERE, man! - to LA BAMBA, drunk on cider in the cricket pavilion at midnight and sang along with MOCKINGBIRD at many a teenage party in my prized summer vacations. The sound of the voice makes me know I'm alive and makes me know that whatever it brings, life is worth living. It is the voice of love.

Dusty's voice has never been equalled or bettered in British pop music for individuality, expression, timbre, pitch or colour. The voice is indefinable except in terms of what it does. It puts whoever listens to it in touch with their feelings. It is an instant conduit to joy, to pain, to laughter or to tears. That aching vibrato, the vocal quiver that sends shivers through the waiting lyrics ... Dusty's vocal performances sear, they soar, sometimes triumphant, sometimes infinitely reflective. She sings and the sound becomes a mirror in which we see all the times we've felt just like her ... The voice rises up, sometimes like a trumpet dancing a descant high over the guitars of a mariachi backing, sometimes like a flute or clarinet in a wildly swinging jazz band, sometimes sounding like the rending of a silk stocking being dragged over barbed wire, sometimes like the same silk stocking floating hidden, just out of reach, in a sea of viscose tears. Instruments make sound and sound communicates mood and feeling. Yearning and longing. Dusty sang a love song like no British white woman has sung one before or since. No wonder those arms and hands flailed like the thrashing whirling of a combine harvester as she milled every ounce of meaning and significance from her songs, almost propelling herself forward to the key change, then the conclusion and finally, the fade ... Oh, those fades!

Would she do it again?

"No! Wey! No. I don't have any serious regrets but there are certain things I'd do differently. Luckily there are a lot of them that I've forgotten but, umm ... I'm glad I did it. I've no desire to KEEP doing it particularly. Just plod on and when things come up ... all the best things come up from left field. Anything I pursue is usually not right for me and then ... But I have to do the footwork and then something comes up that's such a challenge. I'm not really interested in working unless it's something that offers me a challenge ... I want to run a cattery. I'll make it the best cattery in the world. It's for people who're besotted with cats like me who won't worry about them when they go away. I want one like they have in the States where each cat has a person to look after it and a sitting room and a bedroom

and a big run outside, piped-in music and television and a chef..."

Sounds like real life, Dusty. Everything but the choky bits. And talking of performing again?

"It would be very churlish of me to ignore the fact that people have affection for the songs. I'm not like the people who just want to cut it out entirely. If that's all I had to think about then I might feel differently. If I can balance it with the present and possibly the future ...er ... I mean, that's what I'd like to do. If I only had to go out and sing the past, the past, the past I wouldn't do it. I mean, I've been offered that a lot and I absolutely won't do it. It's not healthy for me. I don't ... The past is the past.

A lot if it I'm truly grateful for, but the past is the past ..."

And the future is the future and in it, I for one hope that it is Mary O'Brien who stars and not Dusty Springfield, although I'm sure the diva will feature heavily nonetheless. As I write, Phonogram are preparing to issue a boxed set of four CD's, tirelessly chosen by the indefatigable Mike Gill. Mike was also responsible for choosing the tracks for THE SILVER COLLECTION which Phonogram issued in 1988 and which has sold upwards of two hundred thousand copies, Dusty's best selling album ever. The boxed set will be equally well-received. The Nashville album ... Well, that is the future, isn't it?

Both Dusty and we have got a lot of mileage out of Miss ... Dusty ... Springfield. We who are left no longer inhabit the same world. The sixties are almost as faraway as Neverland. Although there will always be those who make senseless and insensitive remarks about time's unkind passage, these folk are only a fcw and they probably don't buy too many records and they CERTAINLY don't believe in fairies.

"There's a tremendous amount of baggage in being some-one for so long. If people grow up with you and you were very much part of their evolvement as human beings i.e. in the sixties and then you go away, which I did for quite some time - fifteen years or so, more - they grow up, they get older, they get married, they have kids and they sort of retain a place - if they think of you at all - they retain a place for you as you were. They've grown, they've become different people. You come

back, they expect you to be the same person. They forget that they're not but they have this fixed idea and to shake free of that person that ... They still have that vision of you and if you go and sit, I don't know, in Marlowe in a tea room there and the waitress said, 'Well, you have changed, haven't you?' and I thought, 'Well, you bloody have too. Have you looked in the mirror recently?' Yes, I'm different. 'We're both older,' I wanted to say. 'We're both different people', but she still had seen me that way."

Oh, Dusty ... Let her. Let her THINK what she likes. She's never been Wendy, or Peter or Tinkerbelle. She's never flown and she'll never fly. You don't have to worry about what she THINKS because you can't do anything about it. If the woman hasn't flown already, whatever you think isn't going to help her now. Worry about what YOU think. Take notice of the two hundred thousand people who THINK enough of YOU to want YOU to be part of their lives. Think of all that LOVE!

A lot of people have gone out on a lot of limbs for the old Dusty Springfield NOT to have to take the strain anymore. A lot of people have even died. That thing of wonder, soaring on gossamer wings, its mesmerising colours blinding both its pilot and its passengers doesn't have to. It'd done it's days ... Like Freddie Mercury sings on INNUENDO, *'Don't try so hard!'*

If anyone knew, Freddie did. The alter ego and the original were, proudly, one and the same. The idea is for the one to help the other, not to cause problems. The idea is, surely, that Dusty Springfield makes it easier for Mary O'Brien and vice versa. If not, if it no longer works like that, ditch one, Dusty. If it's the only thing you ever do ever again, ditch one.

EPILOGUE

A spoofy and rather silly documentary was made about Dusty's life. About the life of Dusty Springfield. It was made with Dawn french and Jennifer Saunders and appeared as comedy rather than a serious look at the Springfield career. It certainly wasn't an intrusion, an exposé, another chance for the knives to come out, another excuse for the hounds to bay. What, of course, it most unquestionably did is to boost record sales.

After all, as they used to say in those old variety days, the show must go on. The whisper of that top-of-the-bill trouper mentality echoes rather eerily down the years. Perhaps rather wearily too.

"Because I'm still extremely shy and sometimes I can cover it and I can go anywhere. I can waltz through Harvey Nicholls saying, 'Bring me this, bring me that, do this, do that,' but I don't know when it's going to happen. Now, tomorrow I could go to Harvey Nicholls and run straight out again. I've no idea. Usually, when I'm on a roll and doing lots of things that require me to be 'Miss Diva' and there's a lot of activity, I don't have time to retreat from that persona so I can carry it with me to Harvey Nicholls and I don't care if they recognise me or not but they know I'm somebody. Whereas often if I come up to do something from the country and I've been down there a while, I've been slopping around and then I go to Harvey Nicholls, I don't have the same confidence. It's really weird. I have to have been rolled in that persona, stay in it a while, keep it at a certain level and I can do anything and it works great. Everyone's running here, there and everywhere. I'm running here, there and everywhere. It all gets done. But the more I retreat from it again, then I've got to do it all over again and I sort of build up and become that person ... Sometimes my neighbours have a couple of friends in and I won't go down there. I'll go down if

*the friends are not there, but a stranger ... Suddenly the whole
environment has changed...."*

As I write it is November 1994.

As this book is about to go to print, I read in my Sunday
newspaper that Dusty was diagnosed as having breast cancer
earlier in the year but that after chemotherapy and, apparently,
radiotherapy, she is recovering.

I understand that she felt unwell in Nashville whilst
recording. I can't imagine how she must have felt but I have
always been able to smell my own fear and can therefore
sympathise with her. I know that everyday of my life for several
years now, I wake up and check my body, probably foolishly, for
signs of lesions, lumps, moles that are getting too large. I hold
the memories of too many dead friends to be able to ignore what
is the most real threat to our lives, namely that of failed health.
Against the prospect of serious illness or disease, everything
else rather pales into insignificance. What I would do if I ever
found anything untoward about my body in the way Dusty must
have done, I honestly do not know.

Dusty does and for that alone, we must once again salute
her.

Typically, she wanted no one to know. Of course, that
should have been respected but as the state of her health has not
been acknowledge by her management, her record company
and her closest friends and has been documented in the press, I
feel that the process of Dusty's defeating this latest foe, with the
help of the obvious dedication of the medical teams involved in
her treatment, had to be added here.

Once again I have to remark that it is apparent that
anything hidden, anything made or kept secret becomes immediately more sought after. Like the unobtainable being instantly
more desirable, it would seem that privacy is the most impos-
sible bastion to defend for it instantly invites invasion.

It is a heavy price, whatever anyone says.

*"... It's just that old shyness comes through ... I don't
consider it a price. Price is when people get too intrusive. But
... No. It's my job. It's my job. I prefer it when I get paid for it but
there are just times when it's my job ..."*